JUNGLELAND

JUNGLELAND

A MYSTERIOUS LOST CITY,

A WWII SPY, AND A TRUE STORY

OF DEADLY ADVENTURE

CHRISTOPHER S. STEWART

HARPER

www.harpercollins.com

HarperCollins books may be purchased for educational, business, or sales promotional use. For information, please e-mail the Special Markets Department at SPsales@harpercollins.com.

FIRST EDITION

Designed by Fritz Metsch
Maps by Laura Hartman Maestro

Library of Congress Cataloging-in-Publication Data
has been applied for.

ISBN 978-0-06-180254-6 (Hardcover)
ISBN 978-0-06-226699-6 (International Edition)

13 14 15 16 17 OV/RRD 10 9 8 7 6 5 4 3 2 1

For Sky, Dash, and Amy, obviously.

You can believe what you like about those regions: no one has the authority to contradict you. You can postulate the existence in them of prehistoric monsters, of white Indians, of ruined cities, of enormous lakes.

—Peter Fleming, *Brazilian Adventure*

To arrive where we started
And know the place for the first time.

—T. S. Eliot, from "Little Gidding"

CONTENTS

JUNGLELAND

PROLOGUE

THE MAN CALLED himself Rana, or Frog. A machete dangled off his leather belt, and he smoked a cigarette that I'd watched him roll. My three guides suspected that he, like the others who wandered far out here in the Honduran jungle, was a desperado, a convict, or some kind of trafficker. But all he wanted to talk about were the voices of the dead.

"There are people out there," he said. "You can't see them. You only hear them now. The ancient people."

He pointed at his right ear, which glinted in the firelight with a silver stud earring, and his mouth extended into a sly smile, as if he possessed an old secret.

"They are dead, of course. These people."

His cigarette smoke drifted around us in the moist night air. He shook his head. It was early July in the Mosquitia, rainy season, but the rain had stopped, and the two-room thatched hut was alive with noise—chirping, tweeting, burping, groaning.

I squinted through a cutout in the hut: nothing for miles and miles. The closest road was probably two days of walking, and my satellite phone wasn't working.

Frog was probably in his late thirties, skinny and tough, in a red tank top emblazoned with dragons and ripped camouflage shorts, a

scuffed cowboy hat cocked forward on his head. We had encountered him and two of his friends, all armed with rifles and machetes,
earlier that day on a desolate stretch up the Río Cuyamel.

Frog said he was on the run but wouldn't explain what he was
running from or what he was doing now in this remote part of
southeastern Honduras. We didn't want to join him, but we had no
choice; otherwise, we might have been stranded on the Cuyamel for
days. I was on a quest.

For weeks I had been searching for the great lost city Ciudad
Blanca. It is considered the El Dorado of Central America, and
scores of explorers, adventurers, scientists, and government secret
agents have pursued it for hundreds of years—all the way back
to Christopher Columbus and the conquistador Hernán Cortés.
Some died; many got sick or lost, or simply disappeared. Douglas
Preston, writing in the *New Yorker*, once described the lost city as
among "the unanswered mysteries of the world." Paul Theroux, in
his novel *The Mosquito Coast*, doesn't mention it by name but refers
to a "secret city" in the Honduran jungle, inhabited by a secluded
and enigmatic tribe called the Munchies.

I'd never expected to come here. I'd heard the stories about how
the vanished jungle metropolis might actually be the capital of a
forgotten Mesoamerican civilization two thousand or more years
old. I'd heard other equally archaic stories about ghostly spirits that
protect the ruins, indigenous people with ancient secrets, murderous gold prospectors, and an American spy who had claimed in
1940 that he had found the sacred place, only to die unexpectedly
before disclosing the location.

The last story ultimately pulled me into the jungle. The man's
name was Theodore Morde. I had spent months studying his yellowed expedition journals, logbooks, and letters that few had ever
seen. Morde wrote of burial grounds in the jungle; of a bizarre
Indian ritual called the Dance of the Dead Monkeys; of murderers,
runaways, and lost souls; and of the weeks trekking into what he
called the "forbidden region." In time, I grew obsessed.

Now I had hiked more than a hundred miles in military-issue jungle boots with a forty-pound bag strapped to my back. Up mountains, through rivers, sometimes in propulsive rain, other times in burning sun, swinging a foot-and-a-half-long machete at thick vegetation. I was itchy from the bugs, aching everywhere, blistery, and wet. My boots were shot. My back hurt. I stank. I hadn't slept in days, had run out of Valium the night before, and longed for my wife and three-year-old daughter, whose fourth birthday I was about to miss.

Every day came with mortal threats: lethal snakes hiding in the bush, airborne viruses, bullet ants, road bandits, river pirates. The country was in the throes of a military coup, and I had already seen two dead bodies: a motorcyclist lying in the middle of a dirt road and a boy floating facedown in a river. I had never felt so alone. My mind strayed constantly, and my brooding always led me to the same disturbing place: I felt as though I were disappearing. Or, worse yet, that I had disappeared.

"You're a long way from home," Frog said as the rain returned.

I laughed, but he didn't even crack a smile.

"Are you lost?" he asked.

He looked me hard in the eye. He said it was easy to lose your way in the jungle. "Don't follow the voices of the dead," he warned. "That's my advice for you."

I said good night, retreated, and slumped into my hammock, the rain slapping the tarp over me. I looked out at the wet, impassable hell of the jungle and heard my wife's voice over and over again from the day I left home. "What are you thinking? What are you really looking for? Why are you leaving?"

Morning was still hours away, but I couldn't sleep.

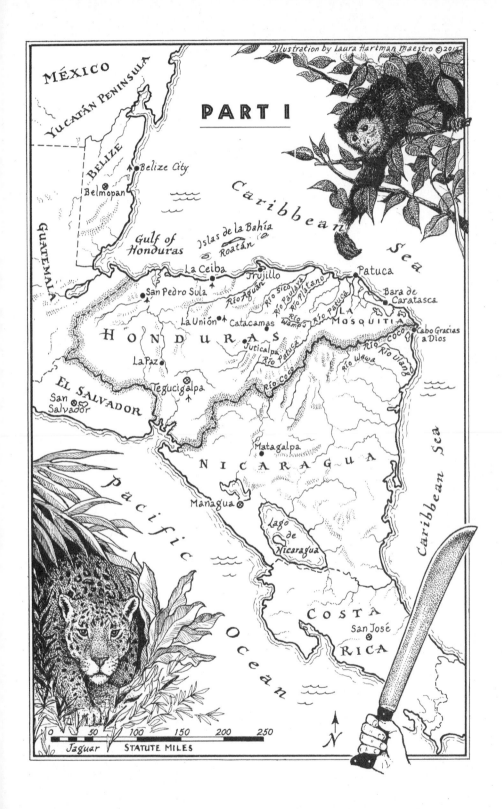

Illustration by Laura Hartman Maestro ©2011

PART I

MÉXICO

YUCATÁN PENINSULA

BELIZE

•Belize City

⊗
Belmopan

GUATEMALA

Caribbean Sea

Gulf of
Honduras

Islas de la Bahía
Roatán

La Ceiba

Trujillo

Patuca

San Pedro Sula

Río Aguán

Río Sico

Río Paulaya

Río Plátano

Bara de
Caratasca

La Unión

Catacamas

Río
Wampú

Río Patuca

LA
MOSQUITIA

Cabo Gracias
a Dios

H O N D U R A S

Juticalpa

Río Coco

Río Wawa

Río Ulang

La Paz

Río Patuca

Tegucigalpa

Río Coco

EL SALVADOR

San
Salvador

Pacific

N I C A R A G U A

Matagalpa

Caribbean Sea

Managua ⊗

Lago
de
Nicaragua

Ocean

C O S T A

San José
⊗

R I C A

0   50   100   150   200   250

Jaguar   STATUTE MILES

N

A PROFESSIONAL AMATEUR

REMEMBER THOSE DAYS, I'd start to say to Amy, my wife, when I was feeling particularly old and melancholy. Remember when we decided one night we wanted to go to Paris and the next day we were on a plane? Remember when we stayed out all night and you broke your heel and we ate breakfast at that diner in the West Village? How many times did we do that? Remember when we lived in that $500 studio in Williamsburg with views of the city and we thought we had it made?

In our twenties, we'd bounced around from apartment to apartment. We'd go abroad at least three times a year, sometimes for Amy's work—she's a contemporary-art curator—other times for my freelance writing. My wanderlust had been born out of my largely sedentary childhood. I had grown up in a rigorously normal town of about 30,000 in upstate New York. We didn't travel much, except for a family vacation every July when my brother, my parents, and I climbed into a Ford station wagon and drove to a beach in Delaware. There was a lake in my town, but with little horizon. The hills had no real vistas, and planes flew past overhead at 30,000 feet. Amy liked to joke that if it hadn't been for her coaxing me into our first trip to Europe together, when we were twenty, I would have never left the

States. We didn't have much to worry about then. We made enough to get by. Now there was little time—or money.

I still traveled as a writer, stringing along interesting assignments—a couple weeks in Iran, where I hunted down rogue military shipments, another couple weeks in the Balkans to search out diamond thieves, and more in Russia chasing down mobsters—but those trips never lasted long enough for me to feel as if I was fully inhabiting another world, living out another life. The assignments provided only an approximation of a sustained adventure. By the time the stories came out in the magazines, I was already back to folding laundry and changing diapers.

Amy and I had been married for six years and had just moved with our three-year-old daughter, Sky, from the frantic crush of Manhattan to sleepier Brooklyn. Strapped with a mortgage and talking about having another child, we were settling down—or trying to. That stuff scared me, as I'm sure it does most young adults, especially those living in New York, where everything is so preposterously expensive. I was getting along in my thirties. I craved something more. Who isn't charmed by the idea that there are still secrets left in the world?

I first learned about the lost city in the spring of 2008. At the time, I was reporting a magazine feature about the growing Honduran drug trade. The jungles and Caribbean shores of Honduras were considered major transshipment points for cocaine traveling from Colombia up to the United States, and the business had created a healthy underworld economy. I was interested in a particular drug king who had apparently made a business of killing off the Colombian traffickers at sea, pilfering the cocaine from their submarines or speedboats, then selling it back home. He was said to live on a fortified hilltop mansion above the sea.

After months of reporting, the story fell apart. One day I heard that the drug pirate had taken one of his speedboats out to sea, this time alone, without his gun-toting army, pointed the boat south, and never stopped. Stealing drugs as a business hadn't turned out to be a very sustainable long-term proposition. The man had made his score, and now, it seemed, he would disappear.

In the course of a phone conversation about the drug trade, though, a former U.S. soldier mentioned the lost city. He had been in the Mosquitia during the contra wars to train fighters in what he described as the "shittiest, buggiest shithole jungle in the world." He'd slept in covered hammocks and tents. He'd always been wet and scratching his welts. "That place was bad, man," he said.

He couldn't remember when he'd first heard about the city, if it had been in the bush or at a seaside bar where he chased women, but the stories revolved around the same reports of gold, priceless artifacts, overgrown temples and buildings, and "monkey gods." "I always thought about going out there to find it," he told me. He had never tried.

Some nights, when my wife and daughter were asleep, I sat at my computer in the living room and mapped the Honduran jungle, shooting Google's satellite camera downward, flying over winding rivers and tightly packed trees that made up one of the largest rain forests in the world. I zoomed until the image coming back was one impenetrable swath of green, and my imagination seized on what lay beneath.

I researched the White City in down moments, when Amy was teaching in the late afternoons or on the weekends when Sky was at ballet or art class. I made phone calls to archaeologists, prospectors, adventurers, and crackpot conspiracy theorists. I found a magician who had been searching for the city for years and told me, "Once you start looking, it never lets you go. It sucks you up." Another man mentioned "ghosts," and an archaeologist named Chris Begley found the city's legend so captivating that he described it to me as "one of the slipperiest and most elusive mysteries."

From what I could tell, the first inklings of a vanished city came from Christopher Columbus when, on his fourth voyage in 1502, he landed in the eastern part of Honduras at a point now known as the city of Trujillo. Walking the beaches nearby, he described in his journals rumors of gold nuggets "larger than lima beans" and an "island made entirely of gold."

But where? Almost twenty-four years later Hernán Cortés and his army of conquistadors arrived on the same eastern spit of land. In his letters home to King Charles of Spain, Cortés described the hunt for the legendary town of Hueitapalan, or the Old Land of Red Earth. His army searched the jungles of Honduras for almost two months but found nothing. Soon after, in 1544, Cristóbal de Pedraza, the bishop of Honduras, wrote a letter to the king about an arduous trip through swamps and forests outside Trujillo. He recalled his introduction to an Indian princess, who had told him of a fabulous civilization west of the sea, "where nobles drank from gold goblets, ate from gold plates." It sounded like El Dorado—one of the original lost-city myths—a golden land ruled by a golden king.

Over the centuries, there were loosely reported sightings. In 1927, on his flight over Central America, Charles Lindbergh spied an expansive stretch of white ruins—"an amazing ancient metropolis." Several years later, an anthropologist named W. D. Strong claimed that he'd found ancient artifacts scattered about the Honduran river basins and that during his six-month expedition, he had heard "many stories of strange archaeological ruins." Not long after, S. H. Glassmire, a mining engineer and gold prospector from New Mexico, announced that he'd found a lost city that was "five square miles," with "crumbling limestone walls." He said that it was overgrown and described walking along a "cornice that stuck out of the ground." Later, his claims were questioned, though they seemed to only stir the seekers.

▾ ▾ ▾

I BEGAN TO daydream about the jungle, about what was under those green Google images, and about all the lavish stories of the lost city. I daydreamed as I strolled past the brownstone buildings of my leafy Brooklyn neighborhood, as I jogged around the paved lanes of Prospect Park, as I pushed my shopping cart through the colorfully stocked aisles of Fairway. At Ikea one Sunday morning, as Sky and Amy tested out a gray cotton pull-out couch, I stood off to the side and let my mind wander. I imagined myself tromping through the heavy jungle air—no iPhone blinking with e-mails and phone calls and Twitter updates. I imagined living off the forest, eating what I caught, drinking river water, my clothes soaked in sweat and rainfall, setting up camp when darkness came, the nights spent listening only to the simple buzz and whir of the forest. No air-conditioning. No aisle 7. No crowds. There I was, in the middle of the jungle, trying to find the lost city by myself. Driving home from the store, I couldn't shake the thought. I drove right past our street and then backed into a sign when I was parking the car. "Sorry," I said. "Just got distracted for a minute."

▾ ▾ ▾

MY CURIOSITY CROSSED into obsession when I encountered Theodore Morde. In 1940, Morde returned from a four-month journey into the deepest parts of the Mosquito jungle with news that he had finally discovered the city. He was only twenty-nine years old. He had already circled the globe five times and visited nearly a hundred nations. As a teenager, he had stowed away on freighters bound for England and Germany. He covered the Spanish Civil War with Ernest Hemingway and George Orwell, lectured on cruise ships, and later worked as a spy during World War II for the Office of Strategic Services, the U.S. intelligence agency that preceded the CIA.

As with many of the great explorers of the past, Morde was more of a seasoned amateur, guided not by classroom study but by guile, boldness, and a tremendous self-confidence. The *New York Times* described his Honduran mission as "exploring hitherto unexplored land" with only a machete and pistol to defend himself. The McNaught Syndicate of newspapers called Morde "a true explorer," as if to suggest that his lost-city discovery made him the last of a special breed of world adventurer.

Morde fascinated me. And it wasn't just his discovery, which would have helped overturn years of science arguing that a major civilization could never exist in such a harsh climate, but also something else: his extravagant life. The fact that he couldn't seem to settle down, that he always burned for adventure.

There was one big problem with the quest of Theodore Morde. Despite his claims of discovery, the city remained a complete mystery. No one knew the location of his city. Fearful that others would plunder the site in his absence, he never actually told anyone how to get to the site, and then he died before he could return to excavate it. His journals and everything else that he had written about the place disappeared after his death. Which made me wonder: Was Morde even telling the truth? And did the city really exist?

At one point I found an article in a 1978 issue of *Sports Illustrated* that detailed an expedition to find the city. Titled "Quest in the Jungle," the story featured two explorers, named Jim Woodman and Bill Spohrer, and mentioned the legend of Morde. I made calls and sent e-mails about the men, hoping that I might find them and that they might give me some more clarity on the legend. I jotted down notes from their trip and added it to my growing notebook on Morde's adventure. When Amy saw my notes lying around the house, she sometimes asked where all this was going. At first I didn't know and I told her so. "Only sniffing around," I said. But soon I started to believe that I was onto something bigger than myself, bigger than anything I had undertaken before, and eventually, despite all the reasons to say no, despite all the trappings of the good life I lived, I just kept wondering—what if? What if I really managed to retrace Morde's journey? What if I traveled to Honduras? What would I discover? Did I have the guts to actually try?

▼ ▼ ▼

"YOU WANT TO do what?" Amy asked the night I told her my plan.

We were having a drink at the dining room table of our Brooklyn apartment one early-winter night in 2008, while Sky was asleep in the back. It was mostly quiet, except for the occasional car that groaned past on the street below and the footfalls of our neighbors overhead.

"I want to find the White City," I said. "Ciudad Blanca!"

She laughed, swallowed a sip of red wine, and, though she'd heard many of my phone conversations with people about the city, searched my face for a sign that I might be joking.

"I'm serious," I said.

"Yeah, I bet the others who went out there were serious too," she said. "How many did you say?"

"I don't know the exact number."

She took a strand of her blond hair and began to twirl it, winding it around an index finger and then letting it go.

"Your hair," I said.

"I can't help it." She let the strand drop. "You don't even know how to camp!" she said.

True: I'm not a backpacker or a trekker or even much of a hiker. I have a bad back. I have lived in New York City for more than fifteen years, so the idea of going to the rain forest might as well have meant heading off to Mars.

"I'm more qualified for this kind of trip," she said before reminding me that she had gone on Outward Bound as a teenager in the High Sierra.

"You were like sixteen," I said weakly.

"Yeah, but I spent twenty-six days in the mountains. And three of those days I was completely alone!"

"Still—" I said, but she cut me off.

"How many days have you spent camping?" she asked.

The answer was probably twice—and I'd hated it both times.

We sat there in silence for some time.

"What about your explorer?" she asked finally.

"Morde?"

"What happened to him?"

"He's dead," I said.

She nodded, as if to underline my obvious lunacy.

"But he didn't die in the jungle," I said.

"That's comforting!"

We laughed uneasily together at that, poured out the last of the wine, and listened as a siren rang out on the street below.

"I feel old," I said as the noise died down.

"Is that what this is about?"

"I'm just saying."

"You're not the only one."

"I'd just like to do this."

"When?"

"Soon, I guess."

"You don't have a plan, do you?" Her green eyes widened. She couldn't believe it. "You've lost your mind. You have."

I told her that there was still a lot to do.

"You and the man-eating, what, jaguars?" she said after some time. "I can just see it."

"They don't eat people," I said. "Jaguars don't."

"Sure they don't. Wait until they see you!"

THE MOUNTAIN THAT CRIES

ARCHAEOLOGISTS SAY THE rain forest is one of the worst environments to dig for human remains. Left to the sodden air, a body is stripped to the bone within eighteen days. The downpours and the resulting streams work away at the crumpled skeleton, breaking it apart piece by piece. The water erodes the bones and ferries them away. Animals take what they want. In a matter of weeks, there is nothing left. The body vanishes.

This is to say that you must want something desperately to even think about venturing into the Mosquitia, 3,300 square miles of relentless nature unfurled along the Caribbean coast between Honduras and Nicaragua. The author Peter Keenagh, who traveled into the Mosquitia in the early twentieth century, described it as "one of the wildest parts of earth."

It is a place of savannas, rolling hills, cordilleras, and many, many swamps. But most of it is rain forest. The jungle is dank and buggy; mosquitoes teem. Trees stand as tall as office towers and in many places block out the daylight. Rivers meander into and out of the fertile gloom. The rain comes without warning, persistent and forceful, a harbinger of some bigger, more malign force that presides out of sight. In places, mountains climb as high as 4,000 feet, with steep intermingling hills packed close like bad teeth. The jungle generates fear. As Theroux put it in *The Mosquito Coast*, "Once you get in, you never get out."

Howler monkeys shriek around the clock, lending the jungle the weird sensation of attending a rock concert. Other strange sounds come and go, sourceless and spectral, without a face. Jaguars prowl, eyes black as asphalt, and bullet ants sting like a .22. The men who roam the forest aren't any better: drug runners, lumber thieves, gold diggers, murderers, outlaws, treasure hunters.

There are stories of downed planes never found again. The natives fear ghosts and jungle spirits that chatter loudly at night and sometimes send messages in gaudy white and purple lights. One of their stories tells of an ugly black witch who guards a pile of gold up a creek off the Río Blanco, in the western part of the country. She preys on men with her striking voice, like the sirens of the *Odyssey*. Sometimes she appears as a beautiful woman with flowing hair that is either blond or black.

▼   ▼   ▼

"I WAS SITTING in a bar in La Ceiba, Honduras, thinking what the hell am going to do?" the explorer Jim Woodman recalled to me one afternoon on the phone.

It had taken me two weeks to track him down. Many of the phone numbers I had turned up online were switched off, and just as I had been about to give up he responded to one of the half-dozen e-mails I'd sent.

"We started talking about the interior of the country with some locals," he said. "From time to time, the Indians would come in with a piece of pottery and try to sell it. I kept hearing stories about this White City. No one went to Mosquitia. It was unexplored. And we thought, 'Goddamn, let's go out there and find this place.'"

It was 1976 then, and Woodman was forty years old. He knew Theodore Morde's story of finding the lost city and wondered if Morde's sudden death had had something to do with the "jungle spirits." He believed in that sort of thing.

Back then, Woodman was still fit from his days as captain of the swim team at the University of New Mexico. Straight and lean as a surfboard, with a mop of brown hair, he was the son of an Illinois newspaperman, had served as a marine during the Korean War, and had then worked as a kind of scout after it had ended—"a destination consultant," he said—for Pan American World Airways, jetting all over the globe in search of new markets for tourism. He married a girl from Rio, and together they had three children and settled in Miami. By the time he felt the pull of the White City, Woodman was a full-time travel writer and explorer who spent much of his time in Central America. He was loose in the world, a kind of hippie without the drugs, but contemptuous of social convention and of setting down roots in one place. He could never sit still.

As he investigated the White City with Bill Spohrer, a Fulbright scholar and archaeologist, they found an old map of Honduras, charted by a local cartographer named Dr. Jesús Aguilar Paz in 1954. To make the map, Aguilar Paz did a lot of walking and talking to the jungle's tribes: Tawahkas, Miskitos, and Pech. At some point, the cartographer met Morde, according to some news reports. His map is curious not for its numerous blank spots—there are a lot of them—but for the tiny black question mark printed near the Pao, Plátano, and Paulaya rivers, next to the words "Ruinas Ciudad Blanca."

Aguilar Paz's marking became the starting point for their adventure, Woodman said. They asked an old friend, Bill Earle, who owned a handful of planes that shuttled people around the country, to fly them out to look for it from the sky. Years before, Earle had left the United States to start a new life in Honduras. But he was afraid of the jungle.

"You're crazy," he told the men. "You have no idea what you're asking. It's loco."

Woodman said he had laughed, not because he thought the response absurd but because he knew an honest warning when he heard one. Earle had already lost three planes to the jungle. Mountains jumped out of nowhere. You'd be flying through gobs of mist and then a piece of rock would appear. Winds shook you up like a soda can. Every trip was a risk, a roll of the dice. But Earle needed the work.

They took his single-engine Cessna for a dozen flights in all. Buzzing over the high jungle canopy, the explorers scanned the sea of green for signs of white. Some days Earle dropped the plane down on a cleared piece of jungle, from which the men would make daylong hikes into the house-high bush. They circled outward from the spot they thought was Aguilar Paz's mark.

They didn't find a thing. When their efforts with Earle failed, they hired a helicopter and traveled in dugout canoes through the winding brown rivers. They carried guns, dehydrated food, compasses, and an extra pair of clothes each. They covered hundreds of miles, though so slowly it felt like thousands, because walking anywhere involved slashing away thick growth with machetes, wall after wall, which occasionally revealed drug runners and lunatics. "We got lost a lot," said Woodman.

Death lurked in the verdure. They discovered two loggers hacked to death with machetes. Their helicopter pilot died in a crash. Occasionally, though, they found clues, reasons to believe that they were closing in on what they were looking for. Shards of ancient pottery with strange markings. Metates, or corn grinders, stuck in the mud. Carvings on jagged granite cliffs along the rivers, like signage on highways, urging them forward.

Along the way, they consulted psychics, snake and jaguar hunters, grizzled prospectors who had logged enough time on the rivers for the rain to ruin their minds. A man who had once owned a rubber plantation on the Río Patuca told them he'd heard a lot of stories about the city, but the thought of actually discovering it frightened him. It's haunted, he said. You'll never come back. Another guy told them that he had been to the city and drunk from a golden mug. A few people told them that they should be looking not for a White City but for a White House. *Casa Blanca*. Or that the city's outer walls, which one man said were as "tall as skyscrapers," were white. Or that, in fact, those walls were simply the razor-edged mountains that rose all around the place.

One year passed, and then a few more. When they weren't working at their day jobs—Woodman as a tourist consultant, Spohrer as an airline operator—they returned to the search. But the more time they spent in the jungle, the bigger the jungle felt to them. They grew tired and dispirited. At one point, ABC filmed a few segments about their exploration. Like many of the explorers before them, they couldn't find a trace.

It was during one of those lean years that they met an old Tawahka Indian woman named Juana. She lived on the Patuca in a leaky wood hut amid a grove of coconut trees. Pigs roamed around her land at the edge of the river and helped keep away snakes. It was hard for the pair to guess her age. Her wrinkled face was a map of her hard life. There were few women like her left. She had never seen a lightbulb.

The men set up camp at the confluence of the Wampú and Patuca rivers, not far from her village. At first, like many tribal people, she was reticent about the city. Woodman told her in his fluent Spanish that he had been searching for the lost city for some time, and she nodded quietly, the river breeze in her matted black hair. Woodman noticed a single gold earring catching the sun. Her nails were unevenly cut.

As the episode was retold in *Sports Illustrated*, she pointed out a high mountain in the distance. It reached into the clouds. "It's there," she said. "You see the white on the mountain?" she asked the travelers. "That is the door to the city. It is the city of the dead."

The explorers stared up at the mountain as the woman looked on. "At night we hear them crying," she said.

"Who?"

"The dead."

"Have you ever gone there?"

She shook her head and looked at him as if he and Spohrer had turned into ghosts. "No one has gone there. You can't."

▼   ▼   ▼

I ASKED JIM WOODMAN on the phone one day if he thought the city existed, because I was still wavering on it. But he wouldn't give me the concrete answer I wanted. "It's a funny thing," he said. "I mean, it's a hard question. Are you going to be in Miami anytime soon?"

I knew from my years as a journalist that there was no substitute for a face-to-face conversation. I had so many questions for him. Most important, I wanted to know what he had found down there.

Amy had an art panel to attend that winter in Miami, and my parents offered to take Sky for a few days. There was still time to change my mind.

▼   ▼   ▼

OVER LUNCH PLATES of rice and beans at a popular Honduran diner in Miami Beach, Jim Woodman told me all about his trip. He wore a faded T-shirt, jeans, and Top-Siders, which he called his "yachtsman shoes." Now eighty, Woodman had lived in Miami for years. He was tanned, with white hair swept back like an old movie star's. He seemed healthy, and his years of tromping around the wilderness still pulsed through him.

He said he had never found it; however, there was a lot more to his story. "I'm glad you came," he said.

From a duffel bag he pulled out an old map, creased and stained, of Honduras, and laid it out on the table. He began pointing on the map to the rivers he had navigated and the mountains he had climbed.

"It's so big," he said of the Mosquito Coast. "It's all off the map." He pointed a rough finger at the Río Patuca and followed the river to a far western part of the country, which at that point didn't mean much to me.

"We went to the mountain that Juana told us about," he said, referring to the old Tawahka woman. "It was white, like she said." He shook his head and tapped the map. "But it was a burial ground. You see them around those rivers and in the mountains," he said, gesturing in the greasy space between us. "Big mounds of earth the size of buildings rising above the jungle."

Over the years he spent exploring the region, Woodman contracted malaria, witnessed men being murdered, got caught in several hurricanes, and survived drug runners and bandits.

"There's an American convict who hides out on that river," he told me. "I don't know if he's still alive. He was hiding out from civilization." He laughed at the thought.

He had found traces of ancient peoples in pottery and statues and discovered an ancient cave inside a white cliff rising like a city tower off the Patuca. "If you go up the river in a low-flying helicopter," he told me, "I'm talking a hundred feet off the ground, and you wind up that river, and go by these incredible walls of white limestone that have openings and many caves. It looks like a white city."

He paused, grew serious. "These were places where the indigenous pre-Columbians lived. We found more burial sites in the niches. That mountain to me—those white outcroppings lining the river—that's the closest we came to Ciudad Blanca."

Woodman, though, has moved on. He writes a travel book every few years—by now he has more than a dozen to his name, one of the most recent about women in the third world. But he did not abandon the search for the White City because he lost faith in the legend. It was just that he'd grown a little restless. As Woodman put it to me that afternoon, "I had spent enough time in Honduras."

About the city, Woodman said, "It was a romance." Such romances are hard to put behind you. "That's the beauty of exploration," he said. "The idea that something like that exists—even if it's an illusion."

We spent two hours together, and before we got up the old explorer leaned over the table, as if he wanted to whisper a secret. He waved one hand. "We can talk about all this in a nice restaurant like this," he said, gesturing to the crowded room. "But you still won't have any idea."

THE MYSTERY STICK

ISTILL DIDN'T HAVE many details about Theodore Morde's trip through the jungle, and part of me wondered if he had been making some of it up. So I began to call around to his remaining family in the hope of shedding more light on the mysteries of his life as an explorer and spy and his journey through the jungle. In time, I got in touch with two of Morde's nieces, as well as one grandchild. All of them pointed me to Dave Morde, Theodore's nephew, in North Carolina.

Up to that point, I hadn't planned to take another research trip, but Dave quickly changed my mind. "I have some files that might help you in your search," he said to me one afternoon on the phone. "A lot of his papers and some other things. Why don't you come for a visit?"

Energized by the prospect of a huge breakthrough in the Morde story, I told him that I would be there in a week.

I flew down to Raleigh, North Carolina, and Dave met me at the airport in his dirt-colored Toyota pickup. Now seventy years old, he is a retired air traffic controller. On his bumper, he had pasted a sticker that wondered, IS THERE LIFE BEFORE COFFEE? As we drove, Dave said, "Uncle Ted was our Indiana Jones."

Dave and his wife, Diana, live in a ranch house in a leafy suburb named Cary. The house is comfortable, with wall-to-wall carpet, lots of cushiony furniture, and photographs of smiling grandkids. We went straight to Dave's basement office, where he flipped on an angled desk light and opened a box. He pulled out a stack of logbooks, maps, news clippings, and journals, all of them worn by time, and some of them flimsily bound together by tape. There was a diary documenting Theodore Morde's Honduran expedition to the lost city. "The family secrets," he said with a smile. Not many had ever seen it. The pages were brittle, yellowed in places, some of the edges ripped and dog-eared. "This is unbelievable," I gushed.

Hours passed as we pored over the journal. Each time Dave turned a page, a musty smell rose up and tickled the inside of my nose. The journals described Morde's way into the wilderness, and I imagined him writing the notes as he floated down the Patuca or as he stayed the night at an Indian village or as he looked out over the valley of Ciudad Blanca.

One thing was still missing in the papers: the specific location of the city. But there were clues—in one passage he noted that the ruins, which included high crumbling walls swallowed up by vegetation, were "between the Wampu and Platano Rivers."

"He was a very secretive man," Dave said when I asked if he thought his uncle had been telling the truth about the city and not advancing a giant fiction. "You know, he was a real spy."

Later, Diana brought us egg-salad sandwiches and a tray of delicious chocolate-chip cookies. When we finished, Dave pulled out a faded piece of paper the size of a diploma and handed it to me. It was his uncle's death certificate.

Morde died in the summer of 1954, and though it was described in his death notice and in the press as a suicide by hanging, Dave and others in the family harbored serious doubts. "He had some very bad enemies," Dave told me. "I like to think someone did him in."

Sadness crossed Dave's face. He had been only thirteen years old when his uncle died, and I could tell the loss still troubled him.

"You think someone killed him?" I asked.

Dave speculated that he might have been killed for his work as a U.S. spy in the Middle East. Or his death could have had something to do with his knowledge of the White City—the spirits that Woodman had talked about. I would later hear this line of thinking from other family members and encounter rumors of his murder online. One web conspiracy theory in particular actually placed his death in London and involved someone deliberately running him over with a car as he planned his return trip to the lost city. At times, the myth of Morde blurred the truth of Morde. What is known is that his life was never the same after he left the jungle and headed to the war. It seemed that he began to question what all of those years of journeying amounted to. Dave suggested that solving the mystery of the lost city might also solve the puzzle of his uncle and why he ended up dead.

I felt a bit overwhelmed about what I was getting myself into.

Now Dave announced that he had one more thing to show me. He disappeared upstairs and came back with the gnarled piece of a wood staff.

"This is it," he said.

I held it and turned it over in my hand.

"This was part of his walking stick," he said. It was darkened in places where Morde had likely held it in his sweaty hands for all those miles of trekking. On the smooth part of the wood was a stamp that read THIRD HONDURAN EXPEDITION. But this was not some mere artifact of sentimental value. A series of coordinates had been etched in knife and ink down the lengths of each of the four sides, as if logging the walking directions to an important place. Some of the combinations read: NE 300; E 100; N 250; SE 300.

I wondered if the numbers might lead me to the center of the mystery.

"Do you think," I asked, "it leads to the lost city?" He thought it might.

I was about to find out.

"TREADING ON DYNAMITE"

THEODORE AMBROSE MORDE'S life changed irrevocably the day he decided to head for the sea. During the first decades of the twentieth century, New Bedford, Massachusetts, was a whaling city, fifty miles south of Boston. There were textile factories too, but fishing was king. Whaling boats crowded the city's salt-stained docks, their hulls faded and beaten, their rudders nicked, and their masts rising stoically against the sky, signs of experiences and survival. Herman Melville set the first chapter of *Moby-Dick* in the city, where he had once worked aboard one of the whalers. "In this same New Bedford there stands a Whaleman's Chapel," Melville wrote, "and few are the moody fishermen, shortly bound for the Indian Ocean or Pacific, who fail to make a Sunday visit to the spot."

New Bedford was then a city where people still made a living from the sea, and some made tremendous fortunes. When Morde was growing up, the population was around 100,000, though the city still felt small, where people knew a face. Morde was a scrawny kid with bushy brown hair. His father, Albert, worked at the city's post office and dabbled at inventing. Among other things, he owned patents for an adjustable carrier strap that would soothe the shoulders of hot dog and soda pop vendors as they climbed up and down the steps of a baseball stadium, and a priming device for internal combustion engines. His mother, Louise, stayed at home to care for Theodore and his two younger siblings, Alice and Elton. Louise was known to be firm. She was a Christian Scientist and preferred suffering over medicine. A teetotaler, she spent whole afternoons inside, or else on the porch, reading the Bible. Albert died of a heart attack at age 69, and Louise lived to be 101. Both outlived their son Theodore.

The family lived in a three-story wood-frame house, coal-heated, with a sweeping roofline, halfway up a steep hill on Pope Street, a block from the water. A cupola provided views of the harbor and the ocean farther off. From up there, Morde could see a good storm blowing in, its swirling blackness, like a pugilist's new bruise, swelling above the water before it came ashore.

A transformation soon overtook young Morde. The exact timing is imprecise. Perhaps it was in middle school, when he was working for pocket change at the local pharmacy and imagining life outside the city, or later on, when he began to linger on the docks, the salty air in his face, reading the names of the ships, watching the men as they packed their boats and sailed off to catch whales, returning weeks or months later, the boats' hulls full of blubber. He heard the fantastical stories of travel and conquest. It was hard to compare that excitement to his own family's settled existence in New Bedford. His father owned a twenty-six-foot cabin cruiser named *Star Dust*. Theodore liked to fish as much as to stare off at the distant horizon and daydream of all the sailors heading off to remote places. What was out there in the world for him? More and more, he wanted to get away and find out.

Sitting in a classroom bored him, despite his interest in books, and Morde kept itching. He graduated from New Bedford High School in 1928 and picked up work at the local radio station, where he became a reporter. Eventually, he enrolled in Brown University, where he studied Spanish and French—until one day he simply disappeared.

The details of his life are mostly murky from that point on. Whether or not he'd been planning his flight is a mystery. He was eighteen or nineteen years old. And for a period of days or weeks, no one heard from him. The rumor among the family was that he'd stowed away on a ship to Germany. There are no records of how he got there, only of his return.

On February 4, 1929, according to a ship manifest, he sailed back in style to New York from Hamburg on the SS *Washington*, a 722-foot luxury steam liner with four masts and two smokestacks. Then one of the most beautiful and opulent ships at sea, she boasted an "electric gymnasium," "electric staircases," and murals and statues inside recalling the life of the first U.S. president.

After that, it was as though he'd been asleep for the first part of his life and was now suddenly awake. He understood something important: his life ran parallel to all the other lives he might lead, other places he might see, so many stories he could one day tell. Later on, his family would talk about his charm, his good looks. But some would also say that once he left New Bedford, he became someone else, an enigma. He could be there with you, laughing and showing you every affection, and at the same time, in his mind, be a million miles away. The day he decided to leave on that ship for Germany was likely the same day that the improbable and perplexing life of Theodore Morde began.

▾　▾　▾

BETWEEN 1928 AND 1937, Morde sailed 250,000 miles and circled the globe five times. It was not a life of comfort, but comfort was not the point. He traveled in crowded, squalid crew quarters, sleeping on bunks or on the floor. The rooms were tight, the air fetid, the ship never still.

Sometimes, he worked as a bellboy, other times as a cook. Some crew members played poker and drank in down moments, but Morde read; he could quote Kipling and kept at his Spanish and French.

The living conditions were worse on the tramps, roaming work vessels that claimed no port of call and followed no fixed schedule. Like migrant workers, the freighters wandered the ocean looking for jobs, and Morde wandered with them. It was nearly impossible to have close friends because people never stuck with the same ship. He endured long stretches alone, but he seemed to enjoy that time. It made him stronger. The sea was his education. After all the traveling, he was no longer a kid. He was in his late twenties. He sent his family telegrams from faraway places with a simple but cryptic message: "STANDBY."

He traveled with a small typewriter and began writing copy about the distant lands he saw; his byline started appearing in Associated Press wire stories, as well as *Reader's Digest*, among other publications. He wrote about confidence men in Paris; a dead man being burned on a pyre in Bombay; cockfighting in Siam. In Nias, a remote island off the western coast of Sumatra, he lived with a tribe of headhunters. He was surprised to find stone houses and paved roads in such a distant place, which made him start to ponder the early seeds of civilization—how does a city like this grow? he wondered. "Where does it get its motive?" he wrote.

By the summer of 1938, he had plunged headlong into the Spanish Civil War, covering the Popular Front's struggle against the Nationalists. He was in good company. The war drew Ernest Hemingway and George Orwell. Morde wandered along with them, among the bombed-out front lines in Madrid and Barcelona, through trenches, and into and out of buildings blasted by enemy fire. "The air was full of tracer bullets, long lines of purple across the blue sky," he recalled later in a lengthy two-part interview with his local newspaper. "With the white puffs of bursting shrapnel it was a pretty, though horrible, sight." He lost fourteen pounds. It was never easy to find a meal, and in time his sleep-deprived and shell-shocked body felt, as he put it, "the tingling sensations of treading on dynamite."

One summer night, when the Nationalist military blocked him from crossing the border into Basque territory in the north, he swam across the Bidassoa River, barely eluding machine gun–armed sentries. "The water was cold, the current was quite fast, but we landed on the other side without mishap," he recalled in the same newspaper interview. "We lay flat on our faces for a few moments, after which, hearing nothing to indicate the presence of sentries, we inched our way through a corn field to a house on the outskirts of Irun. I could have cheered."

There, in Nationalist territory, he disguised himself as a Basque fisherman and made friends with a Spanish spy ring, which helped him navigate the bloodshed. He filed reports detailing the massive casualties, the poverty overtaking the land, and the disturbing rise of "the world's newest uncrowned dictator," Nationalist leader Francisco Franco, a friend and ally of Adolf Hitler. As the months passed, Morde believed he was witnessing the collapse of Western civilization—the rise of fascism and the fall of democracy. He worried that the West, and the United States in particular, was blind to the impending darkness.

The fighting had an intense effect on Morde. At one point, on a small boat that he'd stowed away on in the Mediterranean Sea, he felt for the first time that his life was in danger. Out of nowhere, an enemy military ship appeared. "It was about 4 a.m. when suddenly searchlights were focused on us by some vessel whose outlines we soon discovered to be those of a rebel warship," he said later. "We stayed in the full beam for a full five minutes, expecting them to shell us at any second. Passenger and crew were in a state of hysteria. Personally, I would have given 10 years of my life to have been back in New Bedford," he went on, even though the cruiser eventually moved on "for some reason" without firing. "I wish I had never heard of the Spanish War." All along, he seemed to yearn for another adventure, one that was as exciting as war but maybe not as sinister or political.

▼ ▼ ▼

BEFORE HE FINALLY returned to the United States, Morde got mixed up in a bit of intrigue. In late 1938, Claude G. Bowers, the U.S. ambassador to Spain, wrote an official letter to Spain's minister of state, Don Julio Álvarez del Vayo, about Morde, who, he claimed, "has had a very interesting adventure in which you may be interested." The ambassador recommended that the two meet, describing Morde's intelligence as "very confidential."

The contents of this top secret material and the meeting it inspired are unknown. But the missive is the earliest suggestion of Morde's future life as a spy. In fact, it is possible that by then he had already begun to work as a state operative in at least an informal role.

The notion of a journalist moonlighting as a spook was not exactly far-fetched. Since at least the nineteenth century, governments around the world enlisted reporters and writers as an effective way to get a secret agent into another country. They were skilled at reconnaissance and digging up sources. They could blend into foreign milieus and disappear if necessary. *Reader's Digest* and *Time* were often rumored to be home to U.S. agents during both world wars. Journalists weren't the only ones. Missionaries, geographers, mapmakers, and adventurers too were tapped for espionage efforts. The British government, for instance, was reported to employ explorers from the Royal Geographical Society.

Whatever his relationship with the U.S. government at the time, Morde kept traveling, writing, making radio broadcasts, searching for something, though he never seemed to be quite sure of what. That changed in 1939, on an ocean liner plowing across the Atlantic, when he encountered an explorer named Captain R. Stuart Murray, who told him about the lost city.

▼ ▼ ▼

BY THEN, CAPTAIN MURRAY was already a legend among explorers. Wiry and perpetually tan, with wavy beach-blond hair, he had spent much of his life tromping around the wilderness of Central and South America, searching for traces of ancient civilizations. He was a member of the Royal Geographical Society and the Explorers Club, two of the most prestigious explorer groups in the world, as well as the American Ethnological Society. Camel Cigarettes featured him in a national ad campaign dressed in desert-colored explorer garb and the words: "When I'm trekking through the wilds of Honduras, I like to take a break and smoke a Camel." In interviews Murray cited Sir Arthur Conan Doyle's novel *The Lost World*, likening himself to a character embarked on his own great drama. *The St. Petersburg Times* once described him as inhabiting a "world of poison arrows and blow guns." It was a scary place to be, but Murray told the paper that he was actually more afraid of himself. "The main thing that gets on one's nerves in the jungle is solitude," he mused.

When Murray ran into Morde on the *Stella Polaris* in late 1939, he must have seen a bit of his own wandering self. As the 445-foot boat rolled through high seas, the men exchanged stories about what they'd seen abroad. "I used to sit night after night on the deck of the Stella Polaris talking with Murray," Morde recalled later to the *Sunday Standard-Times*, his hometown paper. Murray was on board as a lecturer, Morde as a writer. Conversation soon veered to Honduras, where Murray said he had recently been on two expeditions.

The U.S. State Department, the Museum of Natural History, and the Museum of the American Indian had sponsored his three-month-long journeys—the first in 1934, the second a year later. The jungle was unpredictable, he said. And fascinating. While traveling, he had come upon obscure native tribes with languages and rituals he did not understand. But the most remarkable part of those journeys had been the rumor Murray kept hearing about a secret ancient city: Ciudad Blanca.

Murray's original mission to survey the unfamiliar land and hunt for artifacts had morphed almost fully into a quest for the lost city. Ciudad Blanca consumed him. At times, he told Morde that he felt he was getting close. He found clues scattered all over the leafy wilderness, like a puzzle waiting to be put together. But among the thousands of relics he carted home, two were especially notable: a small worn stone with eleven hieroglyphic characters chiseled into one side and a miniature sculpture of a monkey shielding his face with his front paws, as if blinded by some penetrating light. What were the makers of those objects saying? He didn't know for certain, but thought that they might have come from the Chorotega, a pre-Columbian group thought to be contemporaries of the Maya. Very little was understood about them.

So there was an obvious question for Murray: Why didn't you go back? If you were so close, why not keep trying?

Saddened, suddenly distant, Murray told Morde that he had always intended to return to the search, but—ahh—life had its way with him. He'd been swept away to other matters. Perhaps Morde would have better luck himself.

When they landed in New York, Captain Murray introduced Morde to the man who had mostly paid for his expeditions. His name was George Heye, and it happened that he was looking for another explorer.

MY LOST-CITY GUIDE

WON'T YOU BE lonely in the jungle?" my daughter, Sky, asked me one night before she went to sleep.

"I'll be fine," I said.

I could see her little eyes blinking in the darkness as we lay on her bed. "You'll be all by yourself," she said.

"There are lots of animals," I pointed out. "They'll keep me company."

"But they might eat you up!" she said, sitting up.

"That's true," I said. "They do have very sharp teeth."

That made her laugh. "Maybe the parrots will be your friends," she said, thinking it through. "They're pretty. They can sing."

"That would be nice," I agreed, and we imagined that together.

When buying my plane ticket to Honduras, I had considered going by myself. I thought maybe it would be more meaningful, that I would find myself. That sounded romantic, in theory, but I realized after some time that the notion of going out there alone wasn't exactly practical. I didn't speak Spanish very well, and there were no road maps for the rain forest. I wasn't afraid of losing myself or being lonely; I was scared of walking in circles and never getting anywhere.

I told Sky that I was hoping I could find a partner to go along with me. "I'll go," she volunteered.

I laughed, said good night to her, and then returned to my computer, where I spent the next hour zooming the Google satellite over the Honduran jungle and firming up plans for my trip.

I wasn't lying about the partner. A few days later, the archaeologist Chris Begley offered to be my guide in the jungle. We had been talking on and off for weeks about the White City and Morde's notes. When I mentioned on the phone that I had a ticket for early July, he said he was going to be there already, leading a river rafting tour. "I can take you through the jungle when I'm done," he said. "No problem."

I got lucky.

Chris had spent more than a decade of his life trekking through the Honduran wilds, living in tents and hammocks, studying the lore about ancient worlds that had been covered up and left behind. He was a forty-year-old from Tennessee, a "good ol' boy" with a head on his shoulders—a PhD from the University of Chicago and a Fulbright scholar in El Salvador. The official Web page for him at Transylvania University, in Kentucky, where he teaches anthropology, describes him as the school's "own Indiana Jones, navigating Central American jungles and searching for ancient cities lost to time." No one knew Honduras better. Even the local scientists brought him inquiries of their buried and lost history.

We met for the first time one winter night at a dive bar in Brooklyn. He was in New York now for an event for his fashion designer wife. Chris stood out among the skinny, sleep-deprived Brooklyn hipster kids in black with angular, mussed-up haircuts. In fact, he looked as though he'd just jumped out of the pages of *National Geographic*. He wore sand-colored fast-drying pants with multiple pockets and a white safari shirt. He is about six foot two, with muscular arms and brown hair turning gray and trimmed military-style. His metal-framed glasses looked hard to break.

He apologized for being late, explaining that he had mistakenly climbed on an express subway that had sent him zooming right past his stop and leaving him three neighborhoods and thirty-three blocks away from the bar. But instead of taking the local train back a few stations, which is what I would have done, he'd gotten out and walked. Chris, I learned, is mostly everything I'm not: he loves camping, doesn't mind being wet, and couldn't care less about bugs. As he sipped a Bud Light, he said, "When I'm down there, it's like two different movies are going on. The one there, with me out in the jungle, and the one at home, with my wife and kids doing their thing. In this one"—he pointed at us in the dim bar light, as if it were the first act of a Hollywood show—"you never know how it's going to end."

When I asked why he had first gone to Honduras, he said that he had actually started his fieldwork in Bolivia. But the highlands there had already been too worked over by scientists. "I wanted a place where I could strike out on my own," he explained. "I liked the idea of searching for the unknown, you know, and there's a lot of that out there. The unknown."

When he says "out there," Chris always means the jungle. About the jungle, he also likes to point out that facts are sometimes obscure. "It's hard to know what is real or not real," he said. "The standards of truth are different. Here it is 'My grandfather told me this story,' versus our sort of evidence."

Chris can talk for hours about earthen mounds, magnet sites (ancient capitals), and indigenous cosmology. Although he is skeptical of the existence of Ciudad Blanca and Morde's story, he finds the legend to be one of the world's great detective stories. Once he told me, a bit cryptically, that Ciudad Blanca "might be discovered only in being lost."

A couple decades ago his obsession with lost cities in Honduras was considered eccentric. "Just after I began my research, someone asked a friend of mine why I was working out here since there was nothing to be found," he recalled, with a laugh. People believed the area was a waste of time. Chris ignored them. "For a long time people thought it was impossible to develop a civilization in a rain forest. But now we know better than that." He smiled. "It is not the counterfeit paradise that everyone talked about."

He was referring to the archaeologist Betty Meggers's argument in the 1960s that although the jungle seemed lush, it was actually a rainy, hot, mushy hell, with little opportunity to do the kind of farming necessary to support a large civilization. Meggers suggested that this unfriendly world could be inhabited only by tiny bands of hunter-gatherers, people who had little attachment to one place over another.

In more recent years, however, archaeologists such as Clark Erickson, of the University of Pennsylvania, and Michael Heckenberger (who appears in David Grann's book *The Lost City of Z*), of the University of Florida, have begun to refute that argument in the Amazon. In field research, the scientists discovered evidence of ancient life in the form of "black earth," or fertilized land, suggesting that advanced farming was undertaken in these areas. Chris said it was that skepticism toward ancient life that persisted in debates he had about Honduras—until he began to document it in the early 1990s. "I did a lot of walking," he said.

Since then, he's discovered hundreds of sites, many of them related, and mapped hundreds of others. He lived with the Pech tribe for five years, sleeping on a dirt floor, and has spent many more years mucking around the wilderness. By no means has he come close to exploring all of it. "No one really has," he said.

As we left the bar that night, Chris said he would begin making plans for our journey and would hire two locals to help carry equipment. "This is gonna be fun," he said in parting.

"I WAS LOST"

INDIANS CALLED GEORGE HEYE Isatigibis, or Slim-Shin—for the narrow legs holding up his colossal body. He weighed nearly three hundred pounds, with a fire-hydrant neck, a gold watch chain across his chest, and a cigar almost always dangling from his mouth. His money came from his father, an oilman who had sold out to John D. Rockefeller. He drove a Rolls-Royce and was regularly seen in New York's finest nightclubs, sometimes, as a friend once said, with a "blond at either elbow and a bucket of champagne in front of him." Long before he decided to go after the lost city, people referred to him as a "boxcar collector," for his impulse to grab up every Native American artifact he could find, no matter how small. Others, though, called him a plunderer, because what he was doing sometimes appeared to be more akin to grave robbing.

Heye's obsession with Indian artifacts began in 1897 on a business trip to Arizona, where, after graduating from Columbia University's School of Mines, he was working on a railroad project in Kingman. For ten months he lived in a tent, and at night he visited the Indians who worked for him. "One night I noticed the wife of one of my Indian foremen biting on what seemed to be a piece of skin," he recalled once. "Upon inquiry I found she was chewing the seams of her husband's deerskin shirt in order to kill the lice. I bought the shirt, became interested in aboriginal customs, and acquired other objects as opportunity offered, sending them back home. . . . That shirt was the start of my collection. Naturally, when I had a shirt I wanted a rattle and moccasins. And then the collecting bug seized me and I was lost." That was a feeling Morde and Murray could relate to.

Elsewhere, Heye described his mission to collect as an attempt to solve "the great mystery of the origin of the prehistoric races of the Western Hemisphere." His critics, however, saw a less elevated man. "He bought all those objects solely in order to own them," an unnamed professor of archaeology told the *New Yorker* in a 1960 profile of the collector. "George was fortified by the sufficient monomania to build up a superlative, disciplined collection."

By the time Morde met him in New York, Heye had truly gotten lost. He was sixty-three and had given up everything—first engineering, then a job on Wall Street—to build his new museum. "George would get himself a new limousine and make a pilgrimage, at ninety miles an hour, across the continent," the professor recalled. "He'd pause at towns that took his fancy, look up the local mortician and the weekly-newspaper editor, and ask for word of people lately deceased, or soon likely to become so, whose possessions might include an Indian collection."

When Heye wasn't out searching himself, he hired scores of anthropologists and adventurers to roam the Americas. "He collected the best anthropologists," the professor continued. "His crew had the money to dig up or buy everything that the rest of us couldn't afford." Early on, he stored his collection in an elegant Madison Avenue mansion, where he lived with his socialite wife (the first of three; his second wife, tired of his artifacts and wandering, would lock him out of his house and ask for a divorce) and two children, but in 1939 it was housed in a four-story building in Harlem, at 155th Street and Broadway, and known as the Museum of the American Indian. (In 1989, the Smithsonian would acquire the entire collection; by that time, the museum had the largest assemblage of Native American artifacts in the world.)

Heye's interest in the lost city was likely owed to an obscure doctor in New Orleans who sold him a stone armadillo decorated with gems. Heye considered it one of the most stunning pieces in his collection. According to the doctor's papers, the armadillo had come from a remote place somewhere in northeastern Honduras, near the rumored location of Ciudad Blanca.

Convinced that there was more treasure to be found, Heye began sending explorers to the area. Before Murray, one of the most prominent had been Frederick Mitchell-Hedges, who had traveled there in 1930 and again in 1931. The press loved to write about his adventures. When the *New York Times* profiled Mitchell-Hedges on his second journey, the story noted that he was seeking the "cradle of race in [the] American jungle." His first trip to the Mosquitia had given him promise. "Within my knowledge," he boasted, "the region contains immense ruins never yet visited, as well as Indian tribes of whom practically nothing is known." The ruins, he specu-lated, "may change the entire scientific conception of the aboriginal races of Central and South America." Mitchell-Hedges's most im-portant discoveries included the sprawling Maya city of Lubaantun, far in the jungles of Belize. There he also excavated a crystal skull, or, as he named it, "the skull of doom," which, in his telling, the Maya high priests had employed "to will death" on their enemies.

But after all his pronouncements, Mitchell-Hedges returned from his second trip some five months later with no evidence of the lost city. Two years after, Heye sent William Duncan Strong, an archaeologist from Columbia University. Strong discovered a grouping of prominent burial mounds along the Río Patuca, which he called the Floresta Mounds. Murray and others followed, sens-ing that they were closing in on a major discovery. But the city re-mained unfound.

Now Murray was handing him Morde. When the two men met in New York, they hit it off and soon made a deal. The giant

Heye grabbed Morde's hand and shook it. It's up to you now, he told him. Whether he knew it or not, Morde had been preparing for this moment his entire life; the journey would be dubbed the Third Honduran Expedition, following Murray's first two attempts. Morde's job, like the others', would be to map the still mostly untraveled interior, document the indigenous tribes, and collect artifacts. The ultimate goal was, of course, to find the lost city.

THE COUP

ON JUNE 28, a couple weeks before I was scheduled to leave for Honduras, a coup broke out and put the trip in jeopardy. That morning, two hundred soldiers charged into the Honduran presidential palace in the capital city of Tegucigalpa. With guns drawn, masked men handcuffed and dragged away the bleary-eyed president, José Manuel Zelaya Rosales, popularly known as Mel.

Like a dangerous criminal, Mel was taken by armored car to an air force base, where he was loaded onto a plane and sent to San José, Costa Rica. There he emerged in front of cameras and declared the coup illegal. "I am president," he said, still in his pajamas. In his absence, the Honduran congress presented a signed resignation letter, later discovered to be a forgery, with the wrong date, and a man named Roberto Micheletti was sworn in as president.

I spent the first few days of the overthrow worrying that Amy would find out and forbid me to go. I was transfixed by the images of chaos online and in the papers: the armed men in smoke-filled streets, the military vehicles rumbling about, the scared Hondurans looking as though they had no idea what would happen next.

The exiled president had apparently gotten himself into the situation by offending elite businessmen and politicians with his populism and close ties to Hugo Chávez, Venezuela's imperious leader.

Mel had been born to a prominent ranching family and was famous around the country for his tall white Stetson hat, cowboy boots, and bushy mustache.

The feeling in some quarters of power seemed to be that he had abandoned his friends—that he had hurt them with things such as raising the minimum wage and opposing the privatization of certain lucrative industries—and was scheming to rewrite the constitution in order to extend his term. Now his old friends felt he had to pay.

As days passed, I kept hearing reports about how hazardous the situation was becoming. The State Department warned travelers to stay away, and some observers worried that the country was on the verge of civil war.

The reckless, danger-seeking part of me grew more excited on hearing such news reports. I kept thinking, perhaps selfishly, how the backdrop of the coup would make for an even better story—not to mention a more intense personal journey. But I also wondered if I simply had a death wish.

When I reached Chris Begley on the phone, he said, "You should be okay getting down there."

"Should?"

"Well, you never know." Then he said, with a laugh, "Very little is ever certain when it comes to this place."

▼ ▼ ▼

HONDURAS — ABOUT THE size of greater Philadelphia, with a population of about 7 million—is one of the least developed countries in the Americas. After Haiti, it is the second poorest nation in the Western Hemisphere. Only about 18 percent of its more than 9,000 miles of roads are paved. It is a rough and volatile place, bursting with desperation: Transparency International ranks it as one of the most corrupt countries in the world, and frequently there are reports agonizing over the country's rising levels of violence.

With nearly seven thousand killings in 2011, averaging about eighteen bodies a day, it is the most murderous country in the world. Many of the murders go unsolved, including most of the 108 Americans killed there over the last seventeen years. As one local man would later say to me, "It's cheap and easy to kill a guy in Honduras. Who is going to catch you? Not the police!"

Honduras borders Guatemala, El Salvador, and Nicaragua, all of which have suffered through civil wars during the past thirty years. There hadn't been a coup in the country since 1982—though there had been almost half a dozen over the course of the previous twenty-five years. The United States has cast a long shadow over the tiny territory for the last century, mainly once the American banana companies arrived and immediately began to dictate how the country would be run. As the former head of United Fruit Company once said, "In Honduras, a mule costs more than a congressman."

During the 1980s, in the midst of the Cold War, the U.S. military set up encampments in the jungle, where they trained the rebel Nicaraguan contras to fight the socialist Sandinistas. Some believe the Americans never left and even today wield influence over Honduran politicians and military. The degree of U.S. involvement in the overthrow, if any, was impossible to know. But in public, the Obama administration was firm in its disapproval of the coup and called for Mel to be returned to power. The United States didn't acknowledge the new president—few countries did—and in fact placed him and his coconspirators on a blacklist, barring them from ever coming to the United States.

I sneaked in moments to continue monitoring the situation online. By the second week, the streets and town squares were brimming with angry Mel supporters—labor union members, teachers, and especially campesinos, or peasants. Tanks prowled the cities, and there were photographs of tear gas exploding in clouds around protesters and police wielding clubs and machine guns that fired rubber bullets.

In the end it was impossible to hide it from Amy. One afternoon, I walked into the living room and saw her reading the *New York Times*.

The front page chronicled the drama. "This is insane," she said. "You know this, right?"

"It's not that bad," I assured her.

"It's turning to war."

"It probably won't," I said.

"But you're still going?"

"The flights are still going," I said. "That means it's not that bad." The last part didn't sound so convincing—and she knew it.

"That doesn't mean you should go."

I told her I'd be out in the jungle, far from the coup. "All that stuff is going on in the cities," I said. "It's quiet in the jungle!"

A day later I read online that the police had started shooting civilians.

"949 MILES TO LA CEIBA"

IN LATE MAY 1940, Morde was on an overnight train from New York to New Orleans, where he would catch a ship to Honduras. He sat in a Pullman car, slumped on a hard but not uncomfortable seat, close to a dusted-over window, the rolling landscape whizzing past but the air inside quiet enough to think. There was so much to noodle: what would he see and find, and would he be a different person when he returned?

By now Morde was twenty-nine years old. He had the posture of a two-by-four and tended to dress theatrically in white suits with wide lapels and string ties. Tall and square-shouldered, he had a frontier face, sharp blue eyes, and the lean physique of a long-distance runner. Typically, he wore his wavy brown hair combed back, slick with a handful of pomade. His deep voice was made for radio. Lots of people told him that. In photographs, he sometimes posed with a rifle, but, no matter what, he always seemed to project that faraway look.

The passengers around him slumped in their own chairs, men in thin ties and women in billowy dresses, sipping soft drinks, their tired faces behind newspapers and books, squinting in the cabin light. It was a hard time for most of them. Over the last eleven years, they had lost jobs and homes and dreams. Now, as the Great Depression loomed large, there was a new concern—another war in Europe. They heard about Joseph Stalin's Soviet army gobbling up Poland, and Hitler preparing an attack on France and Britain. Would the führer come across the Atlantic? War bulletins played on the radio, stories of destruction filled the daily news. They worried that their country would again be swept up into conflict, and what would that mean for their already tenuous lives?

They tried to be hopeful, all of them, clinging to President Franklin D. Roosevelt's promises not to be the world savior this time around, to stay out of battle.

It was hard for Morde to sit still. He was leaving all of that behind. Days before he departed Manhattan, he had written a letter to his parents in Massachusetts, explaining that he was headed "where no white man has been before"—unmapped wilderness on the Mosquito Coast that few knew anything about. He would be gone for four months, and every major news organization was watching one of the most talked-about journeys of that generation: this man headed out to discover a vanished civilization. As a media phenomenon, it was the equivalent of a man traveling to outer space.

Centuries ago, explorers had most of the world yet to discover. But now much of it had been traveled and seen and written about. Ships had circled the globe. The North and South Poles had been reached. The sea had been mined. Mountains had been climbed. There were no more continents to name. Yet Morde remained a dreamer. He had become addicted to an idea that dies hard: that there was something richer out there than the New Bedford in which he had grown up, someplace more beautiful than the sea that he had seen from the decks of many ships, more perfect than any faraway land he'd already seen—a land that could possibly tell us about ourselves, that might even have the power to make us better. He believed that he could find that place.

On April 2, a few days after he'd arrived in New Orleans, he headed straight for the Piety Street Wharf. The reek of brine stung his nostrils as he dodged banana carts and sailors and scanned the crowded docks for his ship, the SS *Wawa*. With him he hauled more than a thousand pounds of equipment, including clothing, cooking pans, candles, kerosene lights, mosquito nets, dynamite, a Luger pistol, and a rifle. He had notebooks for charting rivers and chronicling the natives he met. He had brought a camera to keep a visual record of the journey. He also had a wood walking stick—chest-high, smooth up and down, its handle emblazoned with the words THIRD HONDURAN EXPEDITION—to get him through the tight, tough spots. Once out of the harbor, the ship would sail down the Mississippi, through the bayous, skirting the barrier islands, and then through the Gulf of Mexico and into the Caribbean. Four days later, the *Wawa* would arrive in La Ceiba, Honduras, and from there Morde would voyage on to the Mosquito Coast.

Morde was well aware of the dark fates of the explorers who had gone searching before him. He knew the dangers of trekking into the murk—the thousands, for instance, who had perished looking for El Dorado. He knew the stories of ghosts, of warring Indians, of tropical sicknesses. And he knew he couldn't be certain that he would make it out alive—yet still the jungle drew him.

The city, for Morde, seemed to represent something profound—not just a vanished metropolis, concealed by centuries of moldering soil and lavish vegetation. He imagined an important regional capital, a sprawling city with high walls to fortify it against marauding armies, many buildings and plazas inside, with roads coming and going. A city in the jungle was a grandiose idea, audacious even, challenging the popular view going back centuries that such a developed civilization, with its own economy, politics, and religion, could never have emerged in such an unkind place. And then, if it ever existed, there were further questions to ask: how had it all come to an end, and where had the inhabitants gone?

Wrapped up in all this mystery was another mystery, something even more personal, more elementary to Morde. He was just about to plunge into his thirties. Youth was falling away. Was part of his wanderlust born of anxiety or ambivalence about reaching middle age? Was he feeling the pressures that society put on a man to settle down into domestic convention and make a family? Perhaps he looked at his stable parents, who had been living in the same two-story Massachusetts house for most of their lives, and saw what he didn't want to become, what he thought was too limited. Maybe this journey would help him understand his life better, bring the world into perfect, crystalline focus, the kind of insight that every human being wants.

▼ ▼ ▼

AS HE STOOD on the deck of the *Wawa*, Morde watched workers load the hull with lumber, cement mix, gas, dynamite, and drums of oil. A 1,650-ton steamer, with two hulking smoke stacks and a dinged-up hull, the ship was owned by Standard Fruit Company, which, along with United Fruit Company, controlled the lucrative banana trade between the United States and Honduras. (Decades later, Standard Fruit would become Dole Food Company, and United Fruit would become Chiquita Brands International.) Because it was a working boat, though, there were only a few other passengers, among them a commissary agent and a salesman of cast iron.

There was also Laurence Brown, whom Morde had recruited to come along with him. Brown was an old university classmate, a year older and quieter than Morde. He was tall, with a heavy build, dark buzz-cut hair, and a crooked nose that looked as though it had been broken one too many times. In college, Brown had studied geology and played varsity football. He was a quick thinker with the brute strength of a bull. When Morde contacted him about the expedition, he was working for a company in the oil fields of Texas.

The men made beds in the lower cabin with the other passengers, making sure to keep their belongings close. With the tight quarters, the rolling seas, the gale-force winds beating against the ship, and concern about pirates haunting their dreams, there was no way to get comfortable. They would hardly sleep.

It was 3:30 in the afternoon when the crew finally threw off the thick ropes and picked up anchor and the *Wawa* steamed away from the wharf. Later, as the ship rolled out of the Mississippi and into the bluing Gulf of Mexico, Morde wrote in his journal, "949 miles to La Ceiba."

GOOD-BYE

IFEEL LIKE YOU'RE going off to the moon or something," Amy said on the day I left to find the White City. It was early July, punishingly hot. On the steps in front of our brownstone, Amy and my daughter watched as I headed for the yellow cab waiting at the curb.

I felt a little queasy and wondered if Morde had felt this way when he had said good-bye himself. Amy had come around grudgingly to accepting the trip by now, but her anxiety persisted. She still didn't think I knew what I was doing—and part of me knew she was probably right.

As I threw my bag into the trunk, she stepped down and asked, "Are you sure you have everything?"

The day before, I had spread out my things on our living room floor: two sets of "jungle clothes," which consisted of one pair of pants and shirt for the day and one set for sleeping at night; Tylenol with codeine; Tiger Balm hot pads, to take care of the pain after the marathon walks; Valium, to fight back those anxious nights of being days from anywhere; Lariam, to kill off malaria; iodine, to purify river and stream water for drinking; and a bagful of antibiotics.

In bed that night with Amy, there had been some last-minute discussions about abandoning the trip. "You don't have to do this," she had said. "You could just not go."

"I have to," I said.

"You don't have to do anything."

"I thought you wanted me to go."

"I do, but . . ." Her voice trailed off. Then she turned toward me. I loved her green eyes. When we were first dating in college, I wrote a poem describing them as "bottom-of-the-lake eyes," posturing as the romantic. I wrote her lots of poems then, but I didn't anymore.

She said, "You know, you're not the only one who's trying to figure things out."

I told her I knew that.

"No," she said. "Just know that."

Now, as we stood there on the street, I expected Amy to make some jest about Outward Bound and her being the better camper, but she didn't. She bit her lips. I could tell she was worried about me, about what I would get myself into, especially now that there was a coup. But she didn't say it. She didn't say that she was upset either. She twirled a piece of her hair and said, "Be safe, okay?"

Then Sky bounced down into my arms and said, "I love you, Daddy," and I could have held her like that for hours. "Watch out for the crocodiles," she said. "Remember, Daddy, they have sharp teeth."

We said good-bye, and I stepped into the car. As the taxi pulled away, I realized it would be an eternity before I saw Amy and Sky again. I missed them already, and, for the first time, I thought, You're probably making a big mistake, you're screwing up every-thing that's good in your life.

▼ ▼ ▼

BEFORE BOARDING MY plane, I puttered around the gate for a while, restlessly walking up and down the long corridor, past the fast-food restaurants and magazine shops, battling second thoughts. At one point, I sat across from a family and watched as the man read *Goodnight, Moon* to his baby son. I had read that book to Sky when she was a baby. The family looked as though they were going on vacation, something that I should have been doing instead of heading into a virtual war zone. My chest felt hollowed out, and my head was light. For a moment I considered getting up and walking out of the terminal.

I popped some Tylenol and closed my eyes. My thoughts dispersed with the woman's voice over the speaker announcing it was time to go.

The flight to Atlanta was without incident. But Delta flight 575 from Atlanta to San Pedro Sula, Honduras, was mostly empty, with entire rows of seats without passengers. When I asked an older flight attendant if that was typical for the season, she laughed. "It's not exactly tourist season with a coup going on," she said.

Even with the State Department's recent travel advisory warning Americans to stay away from the country during the conflict, all the flights were still going.

"Let's just hope we can land," the man next to me interjected. He smiled, as if he knew something I didn't.

The week before, the exiled president had attempted to fly back into the country on a jet supplied by Chávez, but the army had blocked the runway with trucks. Rumor had it that he was now planning a return, either dressed as a woman or on a donkey over the mountains and through the jungle.

The pilot throttled the plane, and it charged down the runway. In the air, some of the flight attendants looked a bit nervous about what they would find on the other side.

I slept through the trip. Six hours later the plane skidded onto the runway. San Pedro Sula, Honduras. We were early.

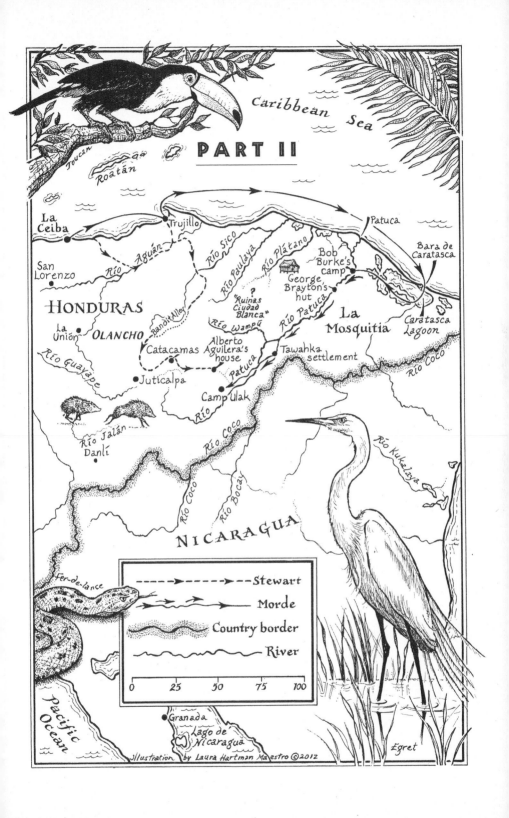

PART II

Caribbean Sea

Toucan

Roatán

La Ceiba

San Lorenzo

Trujillo

Río Aguán

Río

Bandit Alley

Río Sico

Río Paulaya

Río Plátano

?
"Ruinas
Ciudad
Blanca"

Bob
Burke's
camp

George
Brayton's
hut

Patuca

Bara de
Caratasca

HONDURAS

La
Unión

OLANCHO

Catacamas

Río Wampú

Río Patuca

La
Mosquitia

Caratasca
Lagoon

Alberto
Aguilera's
house

Tawahka
settlement

Río Coco

Río Guayape

Juticalpa

Río
Patuca

Camp Ulak

Río

Río Jalán

Danlí

Río Coco

Río Coco

Río Bocay

Río Kukalaya

NICARAGUA

Fer-de-lance

------▶ Stewart

▸▸▸ Morde

Country border

River

0   25   50   75   100

Pacific
Ocean

Granada

Lago de
Nicaragua

Egret

Illustration by Laura Hartman Maestro ©2012

"LEFT FOR DEAD BUT
TOO MEAN TO DIE"

AFTER ALMOST A week of being tossed around at sea, the explorers arrived at La Ceiba, Honduras. It was April 6; the port air was hot and muggy. As Morde and Brown gathered their equipment and lumbered ashore, their muscles throbbed from all the awkward sleeping positions, their heads bursting from the onslaught of the rough waters. They needed rest, but giddiness ran through them like a flash flood. Looking up, they could see the green mountains, angled and curved like a broken rib cage, climbing in the distance before disappearing into a white haze that appeared slightly cursed. Morde wore gabardine breeches, leather boots, and a lightweight shirt. At customs, he and Brown registered their guns; then they headed for the town.

The streets were mostly unpaved, heavily dusted, and dimly lit. There were few electric lights to hold off the darkness pressing in. It was Saturday, and people milled outside—dockworkers, banana hawkers, missionaries, whores. The scene was not unlike the old cowboy West, a place at the edge of civilization, ceaselessly teetering on the verge of chaos. As they walked, they noticed that men carried weapons: guns tucked visibly into their pants, machetes dangling off their belts. There was liveliness in the air, though it was hard to read: a land where you had to watch your back.

La Ceiba wasn't much different from the rest of Honduras, which was going through a stormy moment. The economy, supported mainly by fruit exports, was struggling to get back onto its feet after suffering its own Great Depression. Neighboring countries had dissolved into coups, and the lantern-jawed Honduran president, an ex-general named Tiburcio Carías Andino, was doing everything he could to stave off bedlam. Dissidents were jailed and occasionally executed. A brutal secret police force ranged over the country.

The American banana companies—Standard Fruit, based in La Ceiba and New Orleans, and United Fruit, out of Boston and Tela—had inserted themselves into this political void, and very little happened without their knowledge. They behaved like drug cartels that happened to sell fruit. The companies had muscled their way into most of Central America, with the help of the region's cruelest dictators, and were notorious for their blood-soaked labor fights.

One of the most extreme episodes occurred in Colombia in 1928, about a decade before Morde's trip. It became known as the banana massacre. Banana workers took to the streets to demand more pay and better hours. Military forces, reportedly operating at the behest of United Fruit, which had become known as El Pulpo, or the Octopus, for its wide, sucking strength, opened fire on the crowds. How many died that day is unknown; stories say between forty-seven and two thousand. Later, Gabriel García Márquez would fictionalize the event in *One Hundred Years of Solitude*.

That night, Morde settled down in one of the few hotels in the city—the Paris, a multistory hulk of a building on a public square a few blocks from the sea. There were parrots and palm trees in the courtyard. The jungle was only a few blocks away. Other internationals were also putting up there: hard, grizzled men looking for an angle in the frontier, maybe in bananas or rubber. Restless from their sea voyage, Morde and Brown wandered out for a drink at a rough bar. Still, even with a few drinks in them, it was hard to sleep that first night. Voices from the street kept them awake. So did the temperature.

▼ ▼ ▼

THE FIRST FEW days were enervating. The narcotic heat never let up. It took almost every ounce of their energy to get themselves together and plan out their thousand-plus–mile journey. There was a lot to do. They visited the port looking for boats to take them down the Caribbean coast into the jungle. They went through their equipment, pored over maps, and bought antisnakebite serum made with potassium permanganate. They inquired about guides. Who could help them navigate the wilderness?

As they asked around, they heard about expats living in the river basins: ex-cons who had fled the authorities, dropouts afraid about the war in Europe, prospectors looking to get rich. They heard about some Germans running a plantation and sent word that they were coming.

"The tropics seem to have gotten hold of us," Morde wrote one day in his journal, as if describing a phantom parasite.

A week passed. Morde felt antsy, worried that they'd never get to the jungle. "The Patuca seems so far away," he wrote at one point, referring to the country's longest river, which would deliver them into the deepest parts of the country's interior.

One night, as a diversion, they made a trip to a sparsely inhabited island off the coast called Roatán. A couple centuries before, the island had been home to a reported five thousand pirates who had worked the seas for shipments of gold and silver leaving the Spanish Main, the area from the Gulf of Mexico down to the Caribbean tip of South America. Morde had heard about some ruins in an inland cave.

It was a stomach-turning boat ride through high seas. Wedged between a man and woman "who smelled of goats," Morde couldn't get to sleep. It didn't help that the woman kept throwing up as the boat rose and fell in the swelling waters. When they arrived at the port the next morning, the explorers joked that the boat was appropriately named—*Adiós*. They felt lucky to have made it back onto land.

Talking to locals about rumors of ancient life, they heard about "a great light that blazed up [in the sky] and died down three nights in a row." It had stirred the town into frenzy. What was it? As they stood in the sunshine, a man pointed at the forested interior.

They walked four miles into the bush, looking for the source of the light or some sign of ancient life. When darkness rolled in, they were met by sand flies, which they spent the next few nights picking off their skin. No sign of anything.

Back in La Ceiba that night, they encountered a bloody man outstretched on the dirty street, not far from the hotel. It was late, with few people out. Minutes before, the man had been hacked with a machete, and big red tears of skin flapped from his slender body. Whoever had done it had fled. One hand was completely severed, and his head had been cut wide open, like a watermelon. Miraculously, he was still alive—"left for dead but too mean to die."

If there was any doubt creeping in on them that night, it was soon after replaced by more than a little bit of hope. They located a ship that was going south, and it would take them down the Caribbean coast to Trujillo, the tiny out-of-the-way city in the east that would be their last stop before entering the jungle.

HOTSTUFFIE92

IWOKE WITH A jolt, immediately alert. A gray dawn seeped through the gauzy white curtains. I stared at the ceiling of my room in the Paris Hotel, the same hotel where Morde had stayed almost seventy years before, and I followed the cracks in the plaster as if they were lines of a maze. The night before, we'd arrived at La Ceiba from San Pedro Sula. On the dusty road into town, heavily armed patrols had blocked traffic, a tactic meant to deter anyone looking to cause trouble. At one point, gunshots had filled the soupy air, and I'd sunk low in my seat, expecting my door to be shot out. I sensed that I'd entered a Graham Greene novel, a world of intrigue where anything could happen. I was anxious and a little afraid, and I remembered that early on in his journey, Morde had been that way too.

La Ceiba is now a city of more than 100,000 people, but the docks that once greeted the fruit ships that brought Morde and Brown here slid sadly into the sea years ago. La Ceiba has the typical trappings of a third-world city: ambitious structures from a bygone era crammed next to shacks with metal roofs. Armed guards protect the banks, and the American fast-food restaurants—Kentucky Fried Chicken, Pizza Hut, Popeyes. The streets are noisy with traffic and littered with garbage. The buildings fronting the water are falling down or in various stages of salty decrepitude. Gates, wrapped in concertina wire or topped with broken glass, cordon off the miniature compounds of the wealthy.

The window air conditioner thrummed, holding off the tropical heat, which is oppressive even before the sun comes up. Chris Begley, who had flown down the week before for the river trip, was snoring in the sagging twin bed next to me, unbothered by what loomed ahead. The two locals he had hired to help us on our journey would meet us later.

It was 5 a.m. We would leave in six hours. Like Morde when he first arrived, I was hot and disoriented. I threw freezing faucet water on my face and sorted through my equipment, just to make sure everything was still there. All of my notebooks and maps and pills were packed in Ziploc bags to protect against humidity and rain—and against rivers when we would have no other way of crossing but by plunging in. With all of our food supplies—spaghetti, canned sausages, pancake mix, Tang, coffee grinds—my frame pack weighed about sixty pounds. Chris's monster green army bag was about eighty pounds, jammed with everything I had in my pack, as well as American Geographical Society topographic maps, a GPS, and a bulky satellite phone with one backup battery. The satellite phone was for emergencies, and we hoped that its battery would last us for the full trip.

As Chris slept, I went downstairs to send off some e-mails to family saying I'd made it to La Ceiba and that I wasn't sure when they'd hear from me again. The hotel didn't have many customers because of the overthrow, and the only people up at the time were two straight-faced men in uniforms carrying shotguns, a bored guy at the desk scribbling on a pad of paper, and a flabby black man in a Mets T-shirt and sweatpants plopped down in front of the lobby computer, the one I needed to use.

The Men Without Hats song "Safety Dance" drifted quietly through the fake gray marble lobby. It made me think of a middle school dance, long in my past. A warm nostalgia pulsed through me; it was kind of comforting, an antidote for the loneliness that had already begun creeping in. I felt old again. Where did all those years go?

When I came up behind the guy at the computer, I noticed a window open to a Web site for black singles in La Ceiba, and another window was open to a chat screen, featuring someone with the handle "hotstuffie92." Slumped over the keyboard, he pecked at the keys in slow motion as if weighing very carefully every single letter.

Eventually, he noticed that I was watching and turned. "Is there a problem?" he asked wheezily, moving his body in front of the screen. He appeared to be in his forties. I apologized for appearing intrusive and said I was just curious how long he'd be.

"American," he said, nodding; he clasped and unclasped his thick hands over the keyboard as if he was going to crack his knuckles but decided against it.

He told me he was from Queens and seemed suddenly relieved to be talking to someone else from New York City. "I came to meet some girls," he eventually confessed, pointing at the screen, where "hotstuffie92" awaited him.

I joked that I'd thought single men went to Russia for that. No, he said, it's cheaper to fly here—especially during a coup!—and he thought the women were nicer. He had family from Nicaragua. He'd been to Costa Rica a few times, but it was more expensive to travel there, he said, and "it's like Florida with all those old people retiring there."

He'd been talking to hotstuffie92, a girl from a nearby village, for about a year now. She'd planned to meet him at the Paris, but the military kept blocking the roads, forcing her to turn around. He showed me a creased picture—it had obviously spent too much time in his back pocket—of a dark-skinned woman, slightly over-weight, with a gap between her front teeth. She looked twenty-one years old at most.

"Beautiful," I said. He nodded appreciatively. He said that when she finally got there, he would take her out for a nice dinner. "Maybe Pizza Hut," he said.

He asked what I was doing, and I told him about the White City. Most people I would talk to down here knew about the legend. Locals would invariably refer to the hundreds of square miles in which the ruins were thought to be located as "way out there" or "far, far away," as if the place were located on another planet altogether. The man hadn't heard of the city. He giggled and told me he didn't want to get anywhere near the jungle. He compared it to a kettle of boiling chicken. The closest he'd get to the jungle or any lost city was the pool out back, with the drooping potted flowers and palms.

"I guess we both came here looking for treasure," he joked.

▼ ▼ ▼

WHEN I FINALLY got on the computer, I opened my e-mail to see a note from Amy. She wondered if I had made it. "We miss you," she wrote. As I sat there, I imagined them just finishing breakfast, bowls of cereal, and then heading off for the day—Sky to her summer camp at the school down the street and Amy to an art show.

I replied that the coup wasn't so bad as the papers were making it out to be and that the heat was killing me. I didn't mention anything about the military or the gunshots the night before, but I began to feel sentimental and said that I'd kept thinking about them on the curb as I pulled away in the cab. I told her to tell Sky that an orange parrot lived in the hotel courtyard and that I would call her on her birthday, in about three weeks. "Don't worry about me!" I wrote. As I hit "Send," I realized that this would be the last time I'd have Internet access and thus it would be the last message home.

"WHERE THERE GROW STRANGE
LARGE FLOWERS"

THE TRUJILLO THAT Morde and Brown found was no longer the center of the colonial Spanish Empire. A recent plague had wiped out the city's surrounding banana crops and scattered local laborers to look for work elsewhere, making the place feel barren and remote. As the explorers stumbled off the boat, they walked the same beach that Christopher Columbus and Hernán Cortés had likely walked centuries before. They passed the crumbling Spanish fort, with its defunct cannon. The streets were overgrown with grass, and an eerie quiet suffused the summer air—a "ghost town," Morde called it.

At the top of a sharp hill, the men wandered past a graveyard, where they discovered the decaying tomb of an American bandit named William Walker who had been shot by a firing squad in 1860 for trying to take over the country. The site only made the men more eager to move on.

The visit to Trujillo is really notable for only one reason: Morde's mysterious encounter with a person who claimed to have information about the White City. In his journal, Morde doesn't name the person or even say whether it was a man or a woman. There are no details about where the meeting took place or at what time of day. That person told him that the city was known for its *"arenas blancas,"* or white sands, which proved about as helpful to Morde as the myths Woodman had encountered. As for the city's location, Morde wrote that it might be between the Wampú and Plátano rivers, "over high mountains, where there grow strange large flowers." Under those flowers, this person warned the men, was a burial ground.

▼ ▼ ▼

THE MEN SLEPT uneasily that night, impatient to move on to the frontier. But the next morning brought them some trouble. As they drove to the harbor to find a boat, they accidentally struck and killed a rooster. The timing of the collision couldn't have been worse. Three police officers happened to see it. Drawing rifles, the men stepped into the road and gestured for the explorers to pull over.

The policemen shook their heads at the lifeless bird. "You need to come with us," one of them said.

Morde tried to apologize. The rooster had come out of nowhere, he said. It had surprised them. He wasn't there and then he was. They were sorry.

But sorry wasn't enough. The policemen told Morde and Brown that they were going to jail. They hadn't killed just any rooster; it happened to be the sheriff's prized bird. For a moment, the explorers imagined the worst: the expedition ending in this dead-end town.

At the ramshackle police station, Morde and Brown tried to reason with the sheriff, thinking that he was a reasonable man. But the sheriff just smiled dumbly. He was a big cake of a guy with heavy-lidded eyes. Sweat shone on his face. That was his best fighting cock, he told the explorers, and it had made him money. His hands went up in the air, palms open. What was he supposed to do now without his fighting bird? He wanted the men to make him an offer.

He laughed, and the explorers laughed too. Morde dug into his bag, counted out several gold nuggets, and then dropped them on the sheriff's desk. About $15 worth. That's what it took to stay out of jail.

They headed straight for their ship, the SS *Cisne*, moored at

Trujillo harbor. She was eighty feet long with a strong but battered steel hull, marked up from years at sea. From there she would sail to the easternmost point on the Honduran coast, just north of Nicaragua. Climbing on, there was a reason to be excited. The jungle finally beckoned.

SNAKES AND VALIUM

CHRIS BEGLEY SHUFFLED downstairs. Over eggs and toast in a leafy courtyard we pored over Morde's notes, looked at our maps spread over the round table, and drew up a plan. We wouldn't be following Morde's initial entry by boat from the east, through the Caratasca Lagoon and overland to the Río Patuca. We would instead go along the seacoast, then cut west across the middle of the country on buses and trucks, and from there head by boat to look for Morde's river camps, eventually ending up on the upper reaches of the Patuca, where Morde had been, and then proceed on foot into what Chris described as "the land of the lost cities." Chris pointed to a green mountainous spot on the map in the middle of nowhere. "This is where we'll be heading."

The last time he'd been out there, he said, bandits had kidnapped him. It was one of those moments when he was glad that his wife wasn't watching the real-time movie that was his life in the wild. But he was fortunate. "I found out later that one of the guys had murdered someone and was hiding out." He told the story with evident pride. He had sneaked off in the middle of the night while the men foraged for food. I laughed as if he were joking. He wasn't.

Meanwhile, as we sat there, I realized something disturbing: I'd forgotten my snake gaiters, the nylon puncture-proof polyurethane-coated guards that strapped onto my shins, back in Brooklyn. Snakes seemed to me more dangerous than bandits and even more worrisome than the weird airborne diseases. I hate snakes. Harmless garter snakes freak me out. I tried to get Chris to tell me not to worry. "I'm probably just being crazy about the snakes, right?" I asked.

He shook his head. "No," he said. "They're a very serious concern."

Chris can discuss poisonous snakes for hours, to the brink of madness. He's seen most of them—from the hog-nosed viper to the coral snake. But the most feared is the fer-de-lance—one bite and your blood stops clotting, and you start bleeding from all your pores and orifices, including your eyes. When Chris gets going about the fer-de-lance, his face tightens. They hide in rocks, in trees, in the brush at your feet. Sometimes you see them every day out there. "Once I was climbing a cliff face, and just as I pulled myself up a level I was staring right at one on the rock. Inches from my face," he said. Even with snakebite serum, he went on, you have about eighteen hours to get to a hospital for even a shot at survival. "That means you need a helicopter," he said. And even if you do make it out in time, there's no guarantee you'll live. At the very least, you'll probably lose the leg or the arm that took the bite.

The fear that bolted through me is hard to describe. Before now, I had tried to block out the existence of snakes. Maybe that's why I'd forgotten my gaiters. I had been to war zones and been confronted by mobsters and killers. But this was somehow different. The thought of a giant snake dropping out of a tree onto my neck or a snake chasing me through the jungle freaked me out—it seemed like bad fiction— and then bleeding from every bodily pore for nearly a day sounded worse than the most depraved kinds of torture. I did not want to die by snake.

I asked Chris for ways to protect myself, and he said, "Just stay alert. Do not put your hands down in a bush." Chris had encountered dozens of them over the years and had been lucky so far. But that's all it was for him: luck. Unfortunately, there really was no bulletproof method of staying safe. "Pray," Chris said. I popped my first Valium that afternoon, and, deciding that I wasn't going to rely just on prayer, I bought some soccer shin guards at the local mall.

"DEFINITELY ON THE
WAY AT LAST"

THE *CISNE* **COULD** sleep up to twelve, but the bunks smelled awful. Morde and Brown lay awake at night, worrying about the black clouds shadowing their wake.

The winds grew, and mountainous swells buffeted the ship. The first night, a doctor on board warned that he had heard on the radio about a typhoid outbreak inland. He said that some people had already been evacuated. Be careful, he cautioned them.

Sometimes Captain Cashman turned on his radio, and when the signal was clear enough, there was news of the war in Europe. It continued to unnerve Morde, but the farther he got from La Ceiba and Trujillo, the less interest he had in events across the Atlantic. The war, he said at one time, "seemed far away," the distance of the conflict a relief. Meanwhile, he decided to let his beard grow and began taking quinine for malaria.

When the ship drew within sight of the coastline, there was nothing much to see, just long stretches of white beach, then patches of green, then sandy beach again. No villages. No inhabitants. Here there would be no regular meals, no hotels or beds. All communication with the wider world would soon be cut off.

On April 29, after two days at sea, the *Cisne* entered the Caratasca Lagoon, the first part of a swampy miasma of interconnected creeks, rivers, and lakes that reached twenty-five miles inland and stretched along the coast for nearly sixty miles. It was the gateway to the Mosquitia. The skies still dark, Cashman dropped anchor just off a small village built on stilts. While supplies were unloaded and delivered, the explorers killed time playing the harmonica and poring over maps. They practiced firing their guns, imagining the lethal world that lay ahead.

That night, the *Cisne* sailed deeper into the lagoon, but the boat kept catching the bottom, and Cashman decided that it was too dangerous to risk venturing any farther. The weather would only get worse, and visibility was already nil. Morde contemplated going back up the coast with the ship and disembarking at another point closer to the mouth of the Patuca. At 1 a.m. he scanned the view from the deck. He could see nothing but swampy gloom. The moon was out of sight. There were only brown-black waters, filled with weeds and crocodiles, thick bush rising all around. It was Central America's largest swamp, and it was easy to get lost out there. But if Morde and Brown continued on the *Cisne*, the storm might delay them further, and Cashman warned that there was no guarantee he would be able to dock anywhere along the coast in high seas. They decided to stay and find their own way to the Patuca.

Morde and Brown unloaded more than a thousand pounds of gear onto a stretch of beach and then said good-bye to the old sea captain. As the *Cisne* chugged away, the explorers watched their last connection to civilization fade away, eventually vanishing into the night. Fifteen minutes later, the sky opened up at last, and they shivered underneath a tarp as the rain drummed overhead. In his logbook, Morde wrote, "Horrible night—no sleep. Soaked to the skin." But, he added, with a note of optimism, "Definitely on the way at last!"

THE VALLEY OF THE PRINCESS

WE CAME ACROSS the dead body a few hours into our road trip.

Our rented Toyota SUV was loaded down with our gear. In Morde's footsteps, we were headed east to Trujillo, to which the first rumors of the city had percolated. We planned to stay there the night before meeting the two guides who would take us into the jungle. On the road, we had passed shotgun shacks, gated houses, plantations with fenced-in fields of banana trees and palms, and trash heaps crawling with feral dogs. Soon the houses were fewer and poorer, nothing more than primitive huts dropped into a cutout piece of the greenery. Chris flipped through the Eagles and Bonnie Raitt on the radio while the roads alternated between pavement and dirt and then mostly dirt. At one point, I saw a boy on the side of a road trying to sell an iguana that was at least four feet long and secured on a leash. Every half hour the police or military stopped us, looking for drugs or armed supporters of President Mel.

I had nearly drifted off when Chris pointed out that we were not far from the valley that Pedraza and the princess had gazed across. "There," he said. "You see it?" He pointed at a flat, verdant stretch of land in front of us, covered in African oil palms, and mountains in the distance. I had read the story a hundred times, as it had been relayed in a letter to Spanish King Charles, parsing it for any clues that might help us. Of the earliest tales, Pedraza's was most closely associated with the legend. He had been the first bishop of Honduras. Based in Trujillo, his religious mission had regularly taken him on overnight trips into untracked territories across the country. In his famous journey, a team of sixty "peaceful Indians" had traveled with him for three days and three nights through heavy jungle and swamp before he had reached the top of a mountain. There he had been met by a group of local Indian leaders, including three males and the daughter of a chief. Scholars debate where exactly Pedraza was when his expedition stopped, but most guess that he was between fifty and eighty miles west of the sea.

As Pedraza stood on that mountaintop, the princess talked of a city farther out in the jungle. With a raised hand, she pointed over the valley, where the rolling green land met the blue sky. Over there, she said, is Tagusgualpa—the house where gold is smelted. In the bright sunlight, the golden place shimmered white like the mountains nearby—a white city. In my notes, I had wondered, was this the same place that Columbus and Cortés had talked about? In his letter, Pedraza didn't attempt to estimate how many people lived in the land, nor did he mention the name of the girl's particular city. When pressed for additional details, she said that it was a rich place where people "ate off gold plates," suggesting the home of a civilized people, not savages.

Pedraza's story was particularly gripping to treasure hunters and explorers because he was a respectable priest, not an unreliable and self-inflating conquistador. It was also of interest because the suggestion of such a place complicated the prevailing view that the incoming Europeans were in fact more modern and advanced as a society than the Indians who had been there before. But Father Pedraza never went to the city; at least he never wrote home about it. He returned to Trujillo, leaving the lost city to other seekers.

▼ ▼ ▼

IN THE ROAD, a crowd of people stood in front of an empty school bus that had pulled off to the side. A country song I didn't recognize was playing dimly through a tripartite door that sagged half open. Practically everyone was staring at the ground. We'd almost run them all down, but Chris had veered away and in the same breath told me not to look. He slammed the truck to a stop before we rolled down a swampy ditch. I looked.

Chris stayed behind as I got out and pushed toward the center of the crowd, stepping over a single, carefully polished brown cowboy boot. Another step, and I met the front tire of a motorcycle keeled over on the dirt. Then the man's body.

My mind had trouble synthesizing the scene. The body was twisted up in ways that a body doesn't naturally twist—arms bent back at the elbows, knees loosed from the sockets. Three brilliant white bones shot through the skin of the left and right arms. The man wore blue jeans and a red button-down shirt. His dark hair was wet with blood, and his face was so caked in dirt and stones and blood that it looked like ground beef. The school bus had collided with him head-on and was now parked about five yards up from the scene.

One man stood directly over the body, rubbing his hands into a ball, his face as white as the dead man's protruding bones. I took him to be the driver, a little older than I. The sun blasted down on us, and I thought I could smell the blood. I tasted vomit but managed to stop myself from a full-on retch. I felt dizzy, as if I was going to tip over. The crowd took my gringo stock but otherwise stood impassively, smoking and sipping soft drinks, talking in their familiar Spanish patter. Just as I was turning away, I heard someone say that the biker was only twenty-five, just a kid.

I stumbled back to Chris waiting in the truck, the other Chris, I thought, imagining writing this very scene and going a little nuts. Over the next three days, I would see two more dead bodies, including those of a seven-year-old boy we found floating in a river and a man who had been shot at home. I would think more than

once, "Pray." Chris started the engine, and we drove off through a
swamp to avoid a military blockade. We didn't speak. Trujillo was
some twenty miles away.

▼ ▼ ▼

O. HENRY, WHOSE real name was William Sydney Porter,
wrote about Trujillo in his 1919 collection of short stories, *Cab-
bages and Kings*. In those stories he called Honduras "Anchuria,"
the "land where anything goes," and Trujillo became "Coralio,"
"a little pearl on an emerald band." Nearly three decades before
the book was published, he actually lived in Trujillo for a period
of time—another gringo looking for a way out. It was a rough spot
in his life. He had been a clerk at a bank in Houston when he was
charged with embezzlement, but a day before his trial, he had fled
for New Orleans and then caught a boat for Honduras. "Those
old days of life in the States," he wrote, "seemed like an irritating
dream."

It took two hours driving through the mud for Chris and me
to arrive. Not much has changed in Trujillo since Morde's visit—
and probably little since O. Henry's. The roads are stone or dirt
or a mixture of the two, and you don't have to endure much foot
traffic. There are about 20,000 to 30,000 people scattered around
the central town and the suburbs. The two- and three-story wood
and concrete buildings are brightly painted—blues, greens, yel-
lows. We found an entirely vacant hotel where an older woman
received us as though our arrival was something of an event in the
tiny place's history. My room was on the second floor and smelled
as though the door hadn't been opened in a century. In one corner,
an army of red ants swarmed the stray crumbs of something that
had once been rather large, judging by the distance between the
scattered remains. The top bedsheet was wrinkled in the shape
of a body. A worn Spanish Bible lay on the desk, and there was a
tiny television in the corner that didn't work. In the wall, an air-
conditioning unit sounded as though it was going to shake itself
free, rumbling as loudly as the engine of an eighteen-wheeler.

I tried to call Amy on the hotel phone, thinking that her voice would soothe me, but the machine picked up. It was just about five in the evening in New York, and my mind drifted to them: Sky on the monkey bars down the block, getting in a few final minutes of fun before dinnertime. Or were they on the roof, enjoying the late sun, watering our plants and flowers? I was in a serious daze. "I'm thinking of you guys," I said before hanging up, feeling utterly alone.

When we walked around that evening, most of the town was dark by 9 p.m., as if everyone had gone to sleep. Near the beach, loud country music filled the night air, and we followed it, lured to a pair of restaurants with dueling bass lines emanating from concert-style speakers. But no one was inside either one. Not even a waiter. We strolled past the Spanish fort, which now isn't much more than some crumbling walls, a low-lying stone building, and a few cannon next to some fragrant mango trees. A statue of Christopher Columbus stood on the nearby cliff, pointing out at the dark sea before us. Up a long hill on the way back to the hotel, we ended up at Cementerio Viejo, where the outlaw William Walker is buried. Morde had been here seventy years ago.

We got into a conversation with a woman wearing a loose white dress standing in front of a crumbling two-story building across the street. "Sometimes you see his ghost," she said about Walker. She looked to be in her sixties. In 1860, Walker was captured in Honduras and executed in front of the Spanish fort. He was thirty-six years old. The woman made a gesture as if she was describing a skyscraper. "He is very, very tall," she said about his ghost. "He comes out when the moon is right."

That night I had the shakes. I couldn't get a thought out of my head: this was only my first day. I tried to pray but didn't even know where to begin and fell asleep. When I woke, we were already late to meet our men.

"GOLD FEVER"

BOB BURKE CAME motoring up to Morde and Brown in a forty-foot pitpan, the sort of long, narrow wooden boat that locals used to get around the country's interior. He was a white man but as wild-looking as the boggy foliage around them—scrawny and muscular, in ragged clothes, with a heavy beard and waist-long hair tied back, a blue bandanna wrapped around the crown of his head. He was barefoot. A .45-caliber pistol dangled from his belt like a warning.

That morning, Morde and Brown had made their way up the Caratasca Lagoon to an encampment where natives transported pine out of the jungle. The huts were made of waja leaves, just temporary lodging, and the workers looked rough and frayed as though they'd spent the night brawling over a bottle of rum.

Burke knew the camp owners and had come for supplies. He told Morde and Brown he was from Philadelphia but had been living in Honduras for almost two decades. He shared a hut in the jungle with his Indian wife and their four children about twenty miles inland. He pointed at the swamp. His hut was about five miles from the Río Patuca, and he was heading back there in the morning, if they wanted a ride.

The men spent the night on the beach, where they ate a turtle they had fished out of the water, and, seeing no other options, left with Burke when the sun came up on May 2. The rain held off. As they motored along, the mosquitoes swarmed the air like an aerosol and the foliage slowly came alive. They "saw white and black cranes as tall as man. Egrets by the dozens. White face monkeys in the trees, crocodiles in the creeks." When night fell, the men watched the long inky bodies of crocodiles rise out of the gloom, eyes "gleaming red as rubies."

Burke, in the meantime, filled the silence with the unusual story of his life, which had much in common with the stories of many others who had fled the United States and disappeared into the edges of the jungle. He said he had left Philadelphia when he was nineteen, after an unpleasant stint in the navy. "Under what cloud he left the States, he never mentioned and we never asked," Morde wrote in his journal, though he would later find out that Burke had killed someone over a woman. "He did admit however that he could never go back and that he can't be extradited under Honduras law."

When he landed, Burke said he joined two revolutions in Honduras, smuggling guns from the United States. During the second, he told them, he had been jailed and tortured—machete whipped— over the location of a stash of weapons. That made him laugh. He had refused to tell where it was, and they had eventually released him. The war cache, meanwhile, was still buried in the jungle— because you never knew when another coup was going to flare up. He seemed to imply that the guns represented a kind of insurance policy.

Soon afterward, he'd gone to work for one of the fruit companies, though that hadn't lasted long, so he'd decided he'd rather be on his own. As he put it, he'd kept moving "further and further from civilization until I ended up in Mosquitia."

After marrying, he said, he had taken his family into the bush and treated the experience as an education. He knew the names of most species of trees and flowers—with the Latin designations—and could identify any snake. He said that he "had contempt for the slow fer de lance" and described himself now as an "adventurer and prospector" with a "gold fever that gnaws at the vitals."

It was late in the day when the men arrived at a stretch of hard earth that Morde called Tibalkan Landing, but they still had to trek another four miles through swamp grass and pine savanna to reach Burke's thatched hut. There, Morde was shocked by what he saw. It was "indescribably filthy—pigs snorting around, chickens under foot, also two mangy dogs." The remoteness of the place gave Morde the distinct impression of its being a hideout. But he was too tired and too sore to care; his feet were covered in blisters. He and Brown set up cots outside and slept "like dogs."

The next morning, eager to move on, they hired two horses and a crew of fifty Indians to transport their heavy gear five miles overland to the Río Patuca. When they were ready to go, Burke decided to join their adventure. Anything involving gold interested him. He certainly had the credentials for the mission. He had been up the Patuca, and he'd walked the many surrounding mountains and valleys. He spoke Spanish and every local Indian language, and some of the tribes upriver knew his face. If anyone could help find the lost city, it was Burke. Whether Morde thought twice about having a murderer along with them is impossible to say. But surely a violent streak had its virtues where they were headed. A brutal man like Burke, in other words, could be useful.

PANCHO

CHRIS HAD ARRANGED for us to meet our two lost-city guides at a gas station not far from Trujillo. Pancho and his twenty-one-year-old son Angel had ridden all morning in the back of a battered pickup truck from their tiny village in the far eastern part of the country. When I saw them, at first I was a little confused. It struck me that they weren't exactly dressed for a monthlong journey over mountains, through rain, and into the thick forest. They looked more as though they were headed to the mall. Both wore oversize jeans, leather shoes, and pressed dress shirts. Pancho favored a blue button-down that throughout the trip would always look as though it had just been ironed. He wore a sombrero, Angel a Diesel cap. And they each carried an overnight-size sack, not a giant pack. When I asked about his bag, Pancho just chuckled, as though I were the silly one.

Pancho is solidly built, with a jet-black soap-bar mustache, probably in his late fifties, though Chris told me that he could outwalk both of us. Years before, he had worked with Chris on a dig. He could handle a gun and was a tracker too. "He's a real pro," Chris had said earlier that day. Pancho knew the difference between jaguar tracks and wild pig tracks, and he could calculate how much time had passed since they had been made.

He was also incredibly superstitious. As Pancho climbed into the truck, he said, "Do you want to hear a story about Ciudad Blanca?" I would learn over time that Pancho was a man of few words. You had to listen when he spoke. He didn't repeat himself.

"I was out hunting where people talk about the lost city. It was very far out in the jungle," he said from the backseat as Chris started up the truck. "I had been out there for days, but then I began to get very tired. I had slept but not very much. So I sat down in a clearing, and eventually I fell asleep."

How long he slept, he didn't know. But when he woke up, it was nighttime and he saw a man. "His back was to me, so I couldn't see his face. But it was like he was always there. Like he was sleeping next to me," he said.

Pancho paused and looked out the window at the passing blur of banana plantations. "When I stood up, the man left. I never saw his face. He disappeared," he said.

So who was the man? I asked. Pancho didn't know. "Maybe it was the jungle. The jungle has different forms. Sometimes it is a man, sometimes a woman or even a child," he said. But the man without a face was not his point. His point was that the place we were headed was deceptive. The jungle plays tricks on you. "Do you understand?" Pancho asked. "Strange things happen out there."

▾ ▾ ▾

WHEN CHRIS HAD initially approached Pancho about the trip, he had been hesitant to join us. Not many knowledgeable locals wanted to go where we were going—and for so long. Pancho had other reasons to resist. He had spent a good part of his life in the jungle, and the jungle where we would begin and end our journey, a place known as Olancho, had damaged him. It had stolen many of his friends and family.

Olancho is the largest territory in all of Honduras, about 15,000 square miles of rugged mountains and dense forest. It is larger than the entire neighboring country of El Salvador. For years, it was a place where you could get free farmland. It was too isolated, too buggy, too muddy, and too primitive to appeal to very many.

Still, some like Pancho settled there. "Freedom," he said. He went first with his parents and lived with his seven brothers in a two-room hut they built in two weeks out of pine and palm tree leaves. He fell in love with a woman from the area and soon married her. Later, he constructed his own house. He bought some cows; tilled the land; planted coffee, manioc, and corn, among other staples; and lived off the harvest. He had eight kids, and welcomed more of his relatives who followed his example. For a time things were good. But Pancho's prosperity did not last long. Big ranchers, with their big trucks, moved in, and along with loggers they cut away the jungle. There was no military, no police. The law was fluid—which is still the case today.

In time, two of Pancho's brothers were shot dead. One was killed in a land feud. The motive behind the other's demise is less clear. Pancho moved twice, trying to stay away from village wars and feuding neighbors. Along the way he buried two of his children, who fell sick and died before they could be carried the many miles through heavy jungle to a hospital.

There was a saying about the region: *Olancho es ancho para entrar, y angosto para salir*—Olancho is easy to get into and hard to get out of.

Pancho didn't care to talk much about those days other than to say that it had been a good time and then a sad time. It was hard to leave, but eventually he did. His last home had been in a tiny village called Bonanza. When he moved away for good, he left behind a dream of owning land, of being a farmer, a man with cattle and independent means.

His new house is on the east coast, far from Olancho. Although it was a rental and much smaller, with a lot less land, there were no more greedy ranchers or crazy pioneers. It was a safer place. "I have six children now," he said. "They're all grown up." He smiled at his son Angel, who, like the five others, drove four-wheel-drive trucks of merchandise and passengers up and down the coast.

Over the years, Pancho had returned several times to Olancho, but he had mostly avoided the villages where he had lived. He had not visited most of those places in years. But Chris had persuaded him to come along. Now he headed back home.

▼   ▼   ▼

CHRIS EXPLAINED THE first leg of the trip to Pancho as we drove: we would take a truck straight across the country to the city of Catacamas and then drop down to the Río Blanco, where Morde had set up his main camp. Whereas Morde had made his way up to the Blanco by the Río Patuca, we were going to get there by land and then visit the Patuca later, on our way out. The one road across the territory was about 225 miles long, but it wasn't so much a road as one long dusty creek bed through high, isolated mountains.

We could not take the rental truck either; our rental agreement forbade us from driving to that part of the country, and after thinking about it Chris decided that he didn't want to risk its being hijacked. So that afternoon we dropped it off back in La Ceiba and started talking to drivers about getting over the mountains. The first few men rejected us outright. No one seemed to want to go to Olancho. The one gentleman willing to make the trip asked for $400, more than we were willing to pay, which was his way of underlining our lunacy.

The road was more than just treacherous. In its report about Honduras, the U.S. State Department warns travelers to steer clear of the region: "In Olancho, on the road from Juticalpa to Telica, and from the turn off to Gualaco on Route 39 to San Esteban and Bonito Oriental, rival criminal elements have engaged in violent acts against one another."

Some locals referred to the road as *callejón de los bandidos*, or Bandit Alley. There are stories of carjackings, kidnappings, and murders. Gangs were rumored to hide in the rocky shadows, waiting for targets. A month or so before we arrived, a group wielding AK-47s had reportedly stopped a truckload of people, seized all their valuables, and then shot all of them dead, except for the driver.

After we had spent a few hours talking to taxi drivers and making phone calls, one man finally agreed to make the trip for $100. His name was Juan; he was twenty-six, short and on the flabby side, with shiny black hair sticking up at illogical angles. He had never been on the cross-country road before, but he said he was eager for the experience. He had just started working for a man who ran a network of taxicabs a month before, after years of working in a Pepsi bottling plant. "I am free now and want to see all of the country."

Juan was certain he could borrow a 4×4 pickup, the preferred vehicle of the hinterlands, but the next morning he arrived at our hotel with bad news: the truck had fallen through. It was not, of course, advisable to take the road with anything less than a rugged all-wheel-drive vehicle, but he insisted that we go in his sedan. "*No problema,*" he said enthusiastically, drawing us out to the street. "Good car!"

He wore pressed white jeans and a new-looking baby blue T-shirt, as if he were planning to attend some special event. His teeth were sharply white, and he had shaved his face to a perfect sheen. He smiled a lot, even as sweat dribbled down his face in the hot air.

Out on the street, there it was: a new white Geo Prizm, with tinted windows. It reminded me of the tiny Nissan Sentra sedan I'd had as a teenager—cramped inside, with the suspension of a horse cart. He opened the front door, turned the ignition key, and pointed at the CD player, which was blinking purple. "It's new," he said. "Very loud!"

That was when it hit me that Juan had absolutely no idea what he was getting himself and the new car into. Not only that, the car wasn't even his; it was his boss's car.

"This isn't going to make it," I said, turning to Chris. The wheels were as smooth as pancakes. The car was practically plastic, and its carriage was too low to the ground.

"Well, this is it," Chris said. "We don't have any other choice."

Pancho stood quietly off to the side with Angel, who was making last-minute calls to girlfriends back home.

I shook my head. "And it's too small! It's a fucking breadbox. How are five people going to fit in there and then drive for five hours?"

But we squeezed in anyway, three in the back, me up front, my knees squished against the dashboard. Once we shut the doors, Juan cranked up a reggae mix and made a magician's gesture at the blinking purple lights, as if to say, Can you believe this radio actually lights up? Soon enough we were jetting down the road, heading for the lost city at a swift fifty-two miles per hour.

"THE LAST OUTPOST"

THE TREK TO the Patuca was harder than Morde and Brown had imagined: the rain, the bush, the damn mud. When they finally stopped that night at a tiny camp of Miskito Indians, forty or so miles from the sea, they were wrecked. It was May 3, almost a month after they had first sailed into La Ceiba. "Half our gear is soaked, bags caked with mud, covered in bites," Morde wrote. "So tired."

The camp of about a half-dozen huts slouched along a strip of land on a curve of the river. Compared with the other indigenous tribes, the Miskito are considered relative newcomers to the area—the result of the older tribes of Pech and Tawahka mixing with the English, who had occupied the Mosquitia in the seventeenth century, and the Garifuna, who were the offspring of runaway African slaves. Early on, the Miskito accompanied pirates who roamed the nearby waters. Generally thought to be adventurous, they knew the contours of the sea like the palms of their callused hands.

The explorers asked if they could stay for a couple days, and a family of six took them in. Morde and Brown slept in their hammocks, and Burke took the floor. When they weren't resting, they broke in their boots and walking sticks, tested their rifles, and sought out a boat to take them upriver. From the Indians, they heard vague stories about ancient artifacts hidden to the west and of another

American seeking gold who had died the previous month after a snake bit him sixteen times.

The Indians called Morde "doctor"; he bandaged their cuts, caused by falls and mis-swung machetes, and disinfected some sores, healing acts that were perceived as minor miracles.

The explorers traded salt and sugar for eggs. They ate meals of beans and rice and tortillas, until one night a man surprised them with a white-faced monkey. Jamming a stick through its midsection, the man cooked it over the fire until its skin burned off and its fat crackled.

One afternoon, Morde and Brown decided to do some exploring and trekked away from camp in a northerly direction. Soon they wandered into a narrow box canyon with steep sides that rose high into the sky. On the canyon floor, they stopped at a long, unusual mound of vegetation. Curious about what was underneath, they set about digging away layers and layers of brush and timber. They were encouraged by what they found.

Inside the tangle, large blocks of stone extended some thirty to fifty feet ahead of them. Excited about their find, they excavated and examined the ruins. What were they? Could they be the foundations of ancient structures? Perhaps the footprint of a tiny river village? And if a village, was it related to other villages nearby, or perhaps an outpost of a bigger city somewhere else?

Whatever the ruins were, it was the first sign of ancient life they'd come across on their journey. It was also a very real indication of how easily the wilderness devours everything in it, how over time some things just vanish, leaving hardly a trace of their existence.

▼ ▼ ▼

ON MAY 6, Morde and Brown finally located a boat—a forty-foot mahogany pitpan with a flat shovel bow, powered by a three-and-a-half-horsepower engine. They had to build up the sides another five inches to protect them from the growing rapids. And then on May 7, after packing up and saying good-bye, they set off up the Patuca.

The rain came, the sky almost always the gray color of ruined metal, and the river swelled at times to more than a hundred yards across, quickly turning into a tumult of crosscurrents and frothy churn. Morde steered, while Burke manned the bow and Brown fended off rocks from the middle seat. When the river quieted, the men noticed the ghostly landscape—the flat, unpopulated grass-lands that stretched for miles like the Great Plains.

Somewhere along the way Brown's wristwatch broke. For the Americans, it was the last connection to the civilized world and its schedules. Cutting that tie was probably a good thing, but in their account they attached no larger significance to the watch's failure. They lived according to the cycles of the day, rising with the sun and sleeping when it was dark, just as the natives lived.

A few last expat outposts stood between them and the border-lands that Captain Murray had mentioned and Mitchell-Hedges had written about. Living simply, those dropouts inhabited thatched huts, which they had built with their own hands, at the edge of the world, a remote constellation of outsiders, each man on his own personal journey.

There was George Brayton, a cranky fifty-year-old American. Morde and Brown made it to him after eight hours of paddling and motoring. His two-story hut stood by itself atop a forty-foot bank. It was a home and also a commissary for traffic on the river. "He buys crocodile skins and gold from the Indians and sells them salt, rice, machetes and tobacco," wrote Morde. "He pays the river price of $15 an ounce for gold and sells it for $25. He pays 20 cents per foot for crocodile skins and sells it to a merchant in La Ceiba for 45 cents." His profits, rolled into sweaty wads, were buried in tins around his hut like time capsules, perhaps never to be located again.

Posted on his front door was a sign: EVERYONE WELCOME—EXCEPT EXPLORERS. Brayton lived alone with two colorful macaws he had taught to wisecrack, "Get the hell out of here." Still, he seemed to enjoy company. "He keeps three cots set up and almost anyone is made to feel a real welcome to bed and board," wrote Morde. To the natives, he was Dama, meaning "venerable old man" or Sir.

Every day, an Indian woman from down the river brought him meals while a "bright-eyed little Indian girl" kept his house; he told the men that he was planning to marry the younger one as soon as she learned a bit more English, maybe around Christmas. While Morde and Brown bought a few last-minute provisions, Brayton talked about his old life and how he'd left the States behind because he couldn't find a job. "What good was I back there?" he asked. "No good at all!" On the river, he could "just sit here and the money comes." He didn't miss home at all.

Brayton was not unlike the other wanderers before him who had come to Honduras to find themselves, to forget, to restart—Cortés, Pedraza, Walker, O. Henry. All had left their old lives behind in dreams of transformation—of finding riches or fame or simply something to cover up their past, the way a scar grows over an old wound.

▼ ▼ ▼

A FEW MORE miles upriver, the explorers encountered another American, Will Wood—"half blind and feeble with age." Slumped in a hammock in front of his warped wood shack, his clothes were dirty, his teeth yellow and broken. He didn't want to talk about why he had left Minnesota, why he had decided to become a wanderer, because that was a long time ago. Since then, the damp green air had worked away at his mind.

"Silent green is creeping in on the old man inch by inch, day by day," Morde wrote. "The man is battered by time, by a life spent fighting the jungle, the river and the inexorable lassitude that sucks out a man's guts down here."

The only story Wood told the men was about his dead uncle. Wood had left him behind, like everyone else. But when his uncle had died a few months before, Wood had found out that he had inherited $40,000.

He snickered about that, knowing it was a lot of money. All he had to do was motor out to a coastal town and sign for it.

"Are you going to do it?" Morde wondered.

"Not now," he said, sliding deeper into his hammock, waving his hand at the heat. "I'll go down a little later."

▼ ▼ ▼

BEFORE THEY LEFT the grasslands, the explorers stayed a night with a clutch of German Jews hiding out from the war. They spoke in thick enough accents that the other expats just called them "the Germans." Hardy Feldman, Franz Jeffries, and Mrs. Jeffries were all in their late thirties, tall and blond, and ran a small banana plantation. The Jeffrieses had two small children with them, and there was a drifter who came and went and was known only as Charlie.

Morde was fascinated by their lifestyle. "High on the left bank," he wrote of this unusual family, "three young people try to work out a system of living. Their children have to be taught by their parents, the problems of the community settled harmoniously and the unaccustomed hardships of frontier life accounted for."

Years earlier, the group had purchased the plantation from a western company, but things had not gone as planned. They were sitting on a lot of debt, and their bananas were diseased. When they weren't working the trees, they squatted in front of their one-room shack with its corrugated tin roof and stared out over the river. Their boat had broken down. "They live entirely on credit," Morde scribbled on the night he stayed with the family. "Working, struggling, praying for the day when they can get away."

There was a long history of people trying to exploit the river for riches: loggers, rubber hunters, prospectors. Most of the forays ended badly.

Decades earlier, the banana companies—United and Standard—had started laying train tracks through the country to construct an efficient passage to deliver fruit from the interior plantations to the seaports. Those efforts were soon scotched as the firms learned, in the way that the Spanish had learned centuries earlier, that the jungle resisted development with relentless force.

As soon as the greenery was cut down, it began to grow anew and in no time would be just as densely packed with the high trees, the dangling vines, the snaking undergrowth.

So the jungle and the river through it were graveyards; abandoned prospecting sites littered the edges, as did old mining facilities and banana outposts. Farther up the river from the Germans, for instance, was the sunken wheeler ship *Maid of the Patuca*, which had once ferried prospecting supplies. When the river was low, you could see the ship's ruined iron boiler sticking up from the muck, like a monument to a dead utopian dream. After the boat ran aground, the operation was ditched, and the American entrepreneurs behind the project cut a trail to Catacamas—the small city to the northwest—and sold everything to get back to the States. As Morde wrote of the misadventure, "sic transit Gloria mundi." Easy come, easy go.

That night, the Germans switched on the radio and there was news of the war. According to the announcer, Germany was now attacking Belgium and Holland, while the British army was withdrawing from Norway. Among Morde and his party, there was some momentary concern that the world would be altered in their absence. Morde tried to imagine where the war was headed, where Hitler would go next, but he couldn't get his mind to see it and went to sleep trying to forget it all.

The real adventure began on May 14, just over a month and a half into their journey. In the mountains, the men watched as steep moldering limestone rose up above their narrow boat like "grotesque pillars." Within the jagged cliffs, caves opened up like tiny gaping holes in the earth. The rapids became treacherous at times, which worried the adventurers a bit because the river would grow only more intense. Morde began to sketch maps of the landmarks they passed, marking down the rivers so they knew where they had been. "This is striking country," he wrote that day, his mind imagining all the amazing possibilities ahead. He noted that they had passed "the last outpost of white civilization," and soon the rain forest was everywhere—the trees, the vines, the overwhelming mess of moist vegetation. Anything could happen now. With a mixture of eagerness and trepidation, he wrote, "From now on the interests of everyday existence are of more concern than foreign wars."

BANDIT ALLEY

ON THE WAY across the country, our Geo Prizm began to over-heat, and so did our driver Juan. "Where are we?" he shouted to no one in particular as he veered the sedan to a halt in a scrum of low-lying bushes. We had expected to make that leg of the journey in less than six hours, with no stopping. We were about two thousand feet up a mountainside after almost two hours of driving and two earlier pit stops.

Juan slammed his hands down on the leather-gripped steering wheel and dropped his forehead. The hood looked as though it was hiding a fire, white smoke rising out of its seams. The dirt road had been climbing thousands of feet through hairpins and streambeds and eroded earth that plunged straight into the green abyss. We had passed vehicles left for dead—a pickup in a ditch with no win-dows; a sedan in the pine trees, missing doors. Sometimes SUVs with blacked-out windows zipped past us, likely carrying narcos. Our car had struggled the whole ride. The suspension was shot. I hadn't seen another truck in half an hour.

Juan jumped out and threw open the hood and immediately began to hyperventilate. *"Problema! Problema!"* he yelled. The last time we had stopped was forty minutes before. The radiator was low on coolant, and Juan hadn't brought any backup. He made a sign toward the sky, as if he were either looking for God to help his car along or hoping that the heavens might have an answer for what he was doing out here in this forsaken place.

As Pancho and Chris uncapped the radiator and filled it with one of our last bottles of drinking water, Angel paced in tiny circles with his cell phone raised up in the scorching air, hoping to catch a signal so he could say another good-bye to his girlfriends.

With the sun descending, we climbed back into the car and drove on. For a while, we rode in silence, as if the quiet would make us lighter, cooler, swifter. We passed mud and stone huts with corrugated tin roofs, and then darkness started to usher out the day. Soon there were no more houses. There was nothing, but we seemed to be getting along fine.

Occasionally we stopped to relieve ourselves in the bushes. I was standing at the edge of the road, angling away from the wind, when a man and a woman appeared out of nowhere and caught me in the act. I froze, as if I were poisoning their backyard. Then I put one hand to shield my eyes to make it appear as though I was actually staring out over the valley, a gringo enjoying the sweeping views. They didn't seem to care either way and walked on. I was a stranger here, but only the most recent of my kind.

We made it almost another two hours—climbing higher into the mountains—before the hood started smoking again. The radiator consumed another bottle of water and then another. We had one left. We drove on at a crawl, the car transmission jerking along, Juan swearing in Spanish. It was when the smoking recommenced that I was hit by the terrible realization: the car wasn't going to make it.

"Where are we?" Juan asked as he looked out from under the hood. He had just poured our last bottle of water into the radiator.

No one seemed to know how far we were from Catacamas. Every journey had these moments—times when you were completely adrift, feeling a bit helpless and more than a little terrified, with no clear notion about how a situation was going to play out. This wasn't too far from how I'd felt the day I'd left Amy and Sky in Brooklyn.

"Should I be worried?" I asked Chris.

"Let's not talk about it." He said it without a laugh or a smile.

"But should I?"

"THE EQUIVALENT OF
A STATE SECRET"

IT IS THE equivalent of a state secret," Morde wrote at one point about the lost place.

As the expedition pushed farther into the rain forest, the men prepared to encounter the more remote tribes dotting the upper reaches of the Patuca. Those were the people Morde would have to befriend if he wanted to learn anything about the vast jungle around him.

On the morning of May 15, the men paddled ashore to a Tawahka camp, where blank faces met them. The Tawahkas were one of the jungle's two main indigenous groups—the other, known as the Pech, lived more often in the mountains.

The Tawahkas looked at Morde like the stranger he was—a tall, rangy man visiting from another world. "All politely gazed down from their huts," he wrote.

It was as if the tribe was trying to decide whether to attack or retreat—no different from when the conquistadors had come asking questions. Some carried spears. The women wore threadbare dresses, and most of the men were in pants and T-shirts. The babies were mostly naked.

It was a tense standoff until the chief of the village finally emerged from the brush. In his journals, Morde called him Nicolas; though he was fifty-five, he looked much older, with deep lines stretching across his face. His hair was straight and black. He was short and muscular from years of swinging machetes and paddling up and down the river.

Just as the rain came, Nicolas invited the men up to his hut. His was one of the larger ones, about forty feet long by thirty feet wide, with five low-slung wooden beds inside. Bananas and plantains adorned the wood rafters. In a corner were fish spears, wood bows, and a trough of chichi, a homemade beer brewed from sugarcane and pineapple juice.

The storm continued through the night, allowing the men to dry off next to a cooking fire at the center of the hut. They ate wabul, boiled and mashed plantain with coconut water. At first Nicolas was reticent, but then he began to open up. He said he had fifteen children, the youngest still an infant. Bringing up children in the jungle was a game of chance. He said his people married at twelve and became parents a year later. "We have many children, but many die and are buried in the ground," Nicolas said.

Anthropologists know little about the two tribes, except that they are Amerindian groups with linguistic ties to Panamanian and Colombian cultures. They speak languages in the Chibchan language family, which include speakers from as far south as Colombia. Culturally, the tribes are thought to be similar to people from South America, from whence they likely migrated some three thousand years ago, after war or disease forced them out. Some scholars believe their ancestors were the even more mysterious Chorotega. Before the Spanish invasion, the Chorotega were thought to have been dispersed across Costa Rica, Honduras, and Nicaragua, and they were either distantly related to the Maya and Aztecs or perhaps their contemporaries.

Morde—and Captain Murray before him—believed that the Chorotega had once been part of the lost civilization he sought. "Whether they built the city, or conquered it from an older people and occupied it, is not known," Morde would later write. But the lack of any extensive ruins associated with the group was baffling.

Morde hoped to change that, but when he encountered Nicolas and the other tribesmen, the Indians were dying out as a people. Though their pre-Columbian population was thought to have been in the tens of thousands, if not hundreds of thousands, Morde estimated that the two tribes now numbered in the thousands. Spanish missionaries had converted most of them to Christianity. Now after many generations, they were rapidly becoming exiles from their own land, pushed out of Eden, now on the lam.

As they died out, their history died too. "They have no written language to record the exploits of their ancestral heroes," Morde wrote the night he met with the Tawahka chief. Their entire life, the life that they remembered, was passed down orally. In time, stories became warped, blurred, twisted. There were few hard facts, especially because the Indians were fearful of telling their stories to strangers. Something Nicolas narrated as if it had happened yesterday might actually have happened a hundred years before—or not at all. For Morde, as they wandered up and down the shores of the river and into the surrounding forests, life quickly began to feel less real and more like a tropical romance.

MORTAL THREATS

THE RADIATOR COOLED, and we continued again—in vain. As we built speed and optimism, the Geo Prizm began falling apart. First, a low-hanging branch knocked off the driver-side mirror, and about twenty minutes later, as the rain came in sheets, I looked up to find a crack in the windshield. The road became a muddy stream. The car fishtailed back and forth, huffing up a hill, and a hubcap spun loose. Each time a part flew off, Juan stopped, climbed out, and examined the broken car. Soon he was soaking wet, his chest visible through his blue shirt. When one of the headlights cracked, he'd had enough. Something inside him snapped.

He stepped out of the car, stooped down to the mud, and scooped up the piece of headlight. By now we had been driving for seven hours, and we still didn't know where we were. This was clearly more than Juan had bargained for. Holding the car part up in his right hand, he stared out over the darkening wet valley, as if trying to decide whether to go forward or turn back.

"This isn't my car," he finally said. Even though we were all standing around him in the rain, he didn't seem to notice us. How would his boss react? He had just started the job. I felt sorry for him. I did not want to be responsible for his having to return to his lousy job at the bottling plant.

But there was no time to dwell on such contingencies. "We need to get this car going," Pancho urged. This was especially alarming because Pancho was not one to get excited or to make demands. "We don't want to be out here at night." He pointed at the valley, which was full of shadows. And then he made the universal sign for a gun, put it to his head, and pulled the phantom trigger. The bandits were out there.

Soon Pancho had coaxed Juan back into the car and we were driving again. Night came. For the next hour or so, Pancho sat in the middle of the backseat, his neck craning left to right. He was eyeing the road in front of us as if he had special powers to see into the darkness.

I wondered if Morde had ever considered quitting his trip. But in all of his journals I couldn't remember any such passage. I couldn't get my thoughts to straighten out, so I tried to focus on my daughter, as if the memory of Sky's smiling face would protect me from whatever murderous impulse was out there. I thought of hugging her, the way her little arms just barely reached around my waist, how she held on so tight and sometimes said, "Bear hug, I'm giving you a bear hug." I could use that now, her holding me up.

I closed my eyes but it made me feel only more alone and vulnerable, as if whatever bad thing was going to happen to me was already in the works, fated now, and there was nothing I could do about it. Maybe I deserved to be attacked by masked men with machine guns and machetes.

At the top of a mountain, at about 3,000 feet, a cell phone jingle broke my spiraling thoughts. It was Juan's wife. She had been trying him nonstop after not hearing from him for the last three hours.

At first Juan spoke quietly, and I figured he was trying to explain to her that he was with four men looking for the lost city. Then there was a long stretch where I could hear her clearly berating him. After he snapped his phone closed, he seemed exhausted. "She thinks I'm crazy," he said. I told him my wife thought the same thing about my decision to go on this trip. *You don't have to do this.*

Juan spoke dreamily of his own four-year-old daughter, and I thought dreamily of mine. "I'm going to die," he whimpered.

I had no chance to digest this notion or worry further about my own life because just then two shadows appeared in the road about fifty yards in front of us.

"Watch out!" Pancho yelled.

That was exactly how the bandits took down vehicles: they jumped in the road and set up a circle of guns.

"Turn the car around!" I shouted.

But there was no time to make a U-turn escape. If the bandits had trucks, they would chase us down in a matter of seconds. We discussed accelerating and driving right over them at high speed. Instead we kept creeping forward as if drawn by gravitational force. We were too close to change course now. If they were armed, they could start shooting at any time and we'd be goners. I put my head in my lap, bracing for gunfire.

When I finally looked up, I saw that the shadows were two kids holding up a rope across the road. We stopped, expecting to have to beg for our lives. I said something that didn't come out as anything comprehensible. I pictured the parrots that my daughter had thought might keep me company as I died in this ruined Geo Prizm.

But when the two boys approached, no gunmen followed. Instead, the boys put out their hands. All they wanted was some change.

DANCE OF THE DEAD MONKEYS

WHEN NIGHT CAME at the Tawahka camp, Morde witnessed "an utterly weird ceremony," as he wrote in his journal.

A fire as a high as a house had been lit. The Indians—about three dozen of them—were mostly naked, except for some rags tied around their waists and macaw feathers slung around their necks. All night, they had been drinking chichi, and each now carried the corpse of a spider monkey stuck onto a spear. In the flickering light, their coconut-oiled chests glistened as they danced around a medicine man who wore a necklace of crocodile teeth and baby monkey skulls. As the women and children swayed in the shadows, the men began to cry out along with a drumbeat, a constant *tum-tum* narrating the legend of the Hairy Men, known as Ulaks.

The Indians told Morde that they believed the Ulaks, half men and half spirits, lived on the ground, walked upright, and had the appearance of apes. In his journal, Morde described the legend like this: "One day three Ulaks walked into an Indian village and carried off three of its most beautiful and pleasing maidens. They took the girls back in the caves high in the mountains to live with them and bear their children. From this union came, however, not human nor partly human children but the small Urus (the native word for monkey). And that is why these monkeys are called the 'sons of the hairy men.'" The day before the dance, the Indians had been sent out to kill three monkeys, the equivalent of killing three hairy men. With them, the Indians carried only three arrows to make the three kills. Anything less than three kills in three shots was seen as failure. The dance, then, Morde went on, was "a rite of revenge for the abduction of the three virgins."

As the night wore on, Morde and Brown watched as the ceremony turned into a mass burning—the Dance of the Dead Monkeys. Though the sight of the flaming corpses repelled him, he couldn't turn away. "Under the influence of the fire," he wrote, "the body shakes and quivers as though alive: sometimes it sits bolt upright, or an arm will lift rigidly, a leg drawn up."

The ceremony ended when the last monkey was fully burned. Then a nightlong feast of monkey meat ensued, the tribe getting revenge for their lost ancestors. To Morde, the act recalled the ancient Aztecs, the man-eaters par excellence, who believed that the bodies of their human victims were necessary offerings to appease the gods and maintain the balance of the universe.

What did all this have to do with the secret of the lost city? As Morde pressed the Indians, he began to suspect that the ritual was a "perverted memory" or a mistranslation of the traditions of a distant generation, long before Columbus had arrived. The monkey had perhaps once been a central deity—a monkey god who had a city built for him. Native elders told Morde that "the Monkey god has its priests . . . and perhaps human sacrifices"— but its history remained a mystery, as did the rise and fall of the monkey god's followers.

In parsing the myth, Morde subscribed to a premodern theory, in the mode of Christopher Columbus—that there could be a link between the more advanced ancient civilizations there and in the Far East, where he had once traveled. In the Far East, Hindus worshiped a deity called Hanuman, who was a general among the vanaras, the apelike forest dwellers whose fate it was to battle the demon king Ravana.

What was intriguing to Morde was the notion that the Hanuman myth could have migrated to Honduras ten or fifteen thousand years ago—possibly along with tribes that trekked across the icy northern land bridge known as Beringia, linking present-day Siberia and Alaska.

The idea of people migrating from the east in ancient times—connecting East to West—had a precedent in the so-called lost tribe theory of sixteenth-century Spanish friar Diego Durán. In his book *The Aztecs,* Durán suggested, without any sort of evidence, that Sargon, the king of Assyria in 721 BC, had excommunicated the Ten Tribes of Israel, who had ended up in various far-flung parts of the world, including the Americas. "I cannot help but believe that these Indians are the children of Israel," Durán wrote.

Closer to Morde's own day, a scientist named Lewis Henry Morgan added a twist to the migration theory. In the 1850s, Morgan became famous in the United States and abroad (Charles Darwin cited him) for his social ideas involving the indigenous tribes of the United States. In his studies he claimed that some customs shared between people, no matter how many continents apart, indicated proof of genetic ties. Morde, for his part, thought he saw in the natives along the river "a trace of slanting Oriental eyes and the cheekbones of the Chinese and Hindu."

Few people, if any, these days dispute existence of an early land bridge; however, most scientists have moved away from the idea that cultures were invented in one place, such as Europe or Asia, and diffused to another place, such as the Americas. Every archaeologist now knows that civilizations such as those in Mesoamerica or Andean cultures in Peru, no matter how far-flung, no matter how isolated in the jungles, could spring up entirely alone, self-sufficiently, becoming sophisticated societies from within.

▼ ▼ ▼

WHEN MORDE AND BROWN awoke the next morning, they were surprised by how late they'd slept. The sun was already up, the fog mostly gone. Had the Indians cast a spell on them? Or was it all the

chichi? "Why does it take us so long to get started?" Morde wondered.

The explorers told Nicolas that they wanted to travel to the region
of the "hairy men." Some discussion about that followed, and the
Indians shook their heads. The Tawahkas warned the explorers that
the territory upriver was "to be avoided." The Ulaks, they said, "live
in caves high in the peaks." They urged them not to go.

Whether Morde and Brown voiced their excitement, they likely
took the gloomy reaction as positive news: they were headed in the
direction of the ancient White City. They asked Nicolas for a guide.
Was there anyone who could show them the way? There was much
reluctance, but eventually two stringy fifteen-year-olds stepped forward and offered to help. In Tawahka culture, they were already
men. They knew the land as well as the elders did. They said they
would take the explorers as far as what they called the "forbidden
region."

CATACAMAS

THE LAST COUPLE of hours on the road were silent. Only the sound of the creaking suspension ran beneath our thoughts. We waited for our luck to run out, but nothing happened. Even at the military checkpoint outside Catacamas, the tired soldiers did only a quick search before ducking back inside their trucks.

It was around midnight, almost eleven hours after we'd started out, that we checked into a run-down concrete hotel in the center of town. By then the rain had resumed. As we stepped out, I noticed that one side of the roof of the hotel was warping and looked as if it might collapse in on itself at any moment. But I didn't care about that—we had arrived safely, seemingly through some miracle.

We would never get back the car's hubcap. And though Juan didn't make the return trip that night, I didn't see him the next morning, and I will always wonder how he made it to La Ceiba—if he made it back at all.

Chris and I were assigned a tiny windowless room on the second floor with two stone-hard single beds inches apart. Mine smelled of someone else's body, but I appreciated it, if only for the fact that I needed to lie down. I closed my eyes. The dread was gone, oddly replaced by an invigorated, even emboldened spirit. I felt more alive than I had felt in years.

"We made it, huh?" I said to Chris.

"We did," he said, "Now there's tomorrow, and the next day and the next."

"It can't get much worse than that."

Chris thought that was funny.

That would be the final hotel, the final bed, and the final dry sheets of my journey.

"Get some rest," he said.

"GREEN HELL"

THE OLD PATUCA is a crafty enemy," Morde wrote as the explorers fought their way upstream.

Their two guides, Isidario and Julio, were taciturn as they worked the bow, fending off submerged jungle with their long wood poles, pushing off boulders, and calling out the rapids as they came. It was tough going and physically exhausting. This leg of the trip would last more than a week.

The upper parts of the Patuca were a world abandoned—or never before inhabited. The river edges were bereft of encampments. There might have been people beyond the cliffs that rose steeply away into the tangle of trees and dangling vines, but the explorers didn't see them as they paddled past. Beneath the tall trees and rock faces, the forty-foot pitpan felt like a toy. It made Morde feel insignificant before nature's immensity. There were few vistas.

Morde worried regularly about getting sucked into the rocks at the edges and feared that uprooted trees shooting down the rapids might tear off the bottom of the boat. The closest city was more than five days away. The sudden appearance of boulders the size of cars as the river hurled them near was enough to put the fear of death in Morde. "There are moments of wrath, despair and disgust all at once."

Every day at four o'clock, the expedition pulled ashore and wearily set up camp for the night. A few saplings were cut down for stakes, and waja leaves were used for a roof. Many nights they were too tired to cook. Their joints ached from steering the boat and fighting the rapids. They ate bananas and wabul, which they also consumed in the morning. Soon tiring of the wabul, they decided to hunt game but had no luck for days.

When evening came, they sipped whiskey and smoked cigarettes rolled with their Brown & Williamson machine by the light of a kerosene lamp. Certainly Brown and Morde pressed Isidario and Julio, their Tawahka guides, for stories about significant ruins, though no record of such inquiries survives in the notebooks. On occasion, their minds drifted homeward, and they wondered about the progress of the war and whether the United States had yet entered the fray. When there was nothing more to discuss, they sat "listening fascinated to the sounds of the jungle—cries, screeches, hoots, and crashing of heavy bodies in the brush." Each morning they were off and moving before the sun came up.

In a small notebook, Morde and Brown noted the details of the unmapped realm, the pretty blue-and-orange butterflies, the monkeys calling out, the yellow macaws arcing over the water, the crocodiles basking on the muddy banks, the stray footprints of a solitary human. They also noted their boat speed and compass positions.

The mosquitoes swarmed them, but the ticks were worse, particularly near the shore. "The ticks drop on to your skin from branches and quickly sink their claws into you," Morde wrote. "We average 30 to 40 a day. You have to scrape them out and once out, the procedure is to crush them."

Although the sun made appearances, the rain came most days, the sky turning abruptly black, as if a switch had been flipped. Morde and Brown would soon have to start thinking about taking precautions for the wet season ahead. Flash floods were a concern, waves as high as thirty feet suddenly rising up out of the river and taking down everything in their path. The floods would carry even more abundant debris, scores of ripped-up tree trunks and brush shooting downstream like missiles. Because of the rain, the men were always wet, and a pungent stink of mildew clung to their clothing. They stopped expecting their boots to dry. Their beards grew thick and the heat got to them. "If this is the tropics," Morde wrote, "we'll take Alaska."

Some days seemed to never end. On May 24, nearly a week after leaving the last Tawahka encampment, Morde noted a mounting sense of isolation. The myth of the monkey god occasionally haunted him, as if the verdurous air was slowly affecting his brain. One day, he shot a howler monkey—a son of the race of hairy men—out of a tree for its meat. But once the men reeled the monkey into the boat, Morde admitted to experiencing a feeling of guilt. There was something about the monkey's face that reminded him of a dead relative, and its eyes, which would not shut, seemed to be "looking into my soul." He abandoned the furry carcass to the river.

▼ ▼ ▼

SOMETIMES THE TWO men wondered about the unknowable Burke. Why had he killed a man? Would he do it again? No one asked him. As the expedition pushed farther into the wild, they seemed content that he was on their side. "To see him plunge into the snake infested green hell barefooted gave us courage," Morde mused on one occasion. "Not to do likewise but at least not fear the bush."

There were moments when the jungle seemed to consciously push back at them. Fire ants rose up and invaded camp one night; a squad of a dozen swinging monkeys hurled branches down as their boat passed under the canopies. Another day, a herd of several hundred wild pigs, known as wari, attacked them during a reconnaissance trek into the brush.

Hezekiah Butterworth, an explorer in Nicaragua around the same time, once noted that you could hear the wari coming by the "savage sound of [their] teeth" and that they "moved hither and thither, as though hung on wires." The pigs were known to travel in packs to protect themselves from jaguars and would strike if they felt they were in danger.

One afternoon, the men killed six wari. In the hot sun, the odor of the blood was, as Morde put it, "distressing."

"We are cut and bruised and tired and hungry," Morde wrote after a particularly taxing day. By now, they had run out of whiskey and tobacco and had taken to smoking raw puro leaves. "We talked about strawberry shortcake and ice cream to keep up our spirits."

Soon Isidario and Julio began to talk of turning back. The expedition was about to enter the so-called forbidden region. They turned off the Patuca and were on the Cuyamel, a smaller interior river, with soaring box canyons and cold mountain water.

In late May, seven weeks since they had begun, the explorers arrived at the confluence of the Cuyamel and Blanco rivers. They were about two hundred miles from the coast, far beyond any map or guidance they had taken from Captain Murray. "White men have never before penetrated this far up the river," Burke told the men. The remoteness of the place was both hopeful and disquieting. The Indians agonized openly about evil spirits and warned the party that it was not a savory place to explore, but Morde and Brown were determined. They bade good-bye to the Indians and told them that they would see them when they returned. "In six hours, they had made a raft from the logs of the buoyant balsa wood and floated off downstream, leaving us to explore and face the dangers of Ulak Land alone," Morde recalled.

Morde, Brown, and Burke settled on a raised piece of land along a creek just off the Blanco and built camp in three days of concentrated labor. It made sense for them to stop here—it was in the middle of the Indians' so-called forbidden region, the land they hoped was home to the famous lost city. They macheted away seventy-five square feet of jungle, and on the razed patch they built three open-walled huts—one for sleeping, one for a writing desk, and the last for a kitchen, where a fire would burn. In photographs, the huts appear sturdy and primitive, though also idyllic, like something out of *Robinson Crusoe*. Each was about twenty by twelve feet, constructed from tree branches and waja leaves, and bound together with strips of vine and bark.

Morde dubbed the camp Ulak, after the creek and the hairy men for which the creek was named. It was from there that the expedition would finally begin the search for the ruins, as well as commence some gold prospecting.

By now Morde, Brown, and Burke had each lost about twenty pounds, and their beards itched in the heat and stank in the rain. "It is fortunate that we have each other's company," Morde wrote. At night, the men sang along with a harmonica, played bridge, and often dwelled on "the possibility of gold" that waited for them in the distance like a giant question mark.

LOCO MEN

THE NEXT FEW days I don't fully remember.

We were up at 5 a.m. In Catacamas we bought four machetes, sharpened them, and then squeezed into a banged-up yellow-and-black school bus that looked like something out of *Mad Max*, with roll bars and heavily treaded tires. The bus took us southeast toward the Río Blanco, where we planned to find the site of Morde's Ulak camp. Above the driver's head of stringy black hair, a paper listed the "bus rules," including my favorite: "Please be kind and keep this bus clean. Throw your garbage out the window."

A girl who must have been in her teens sat in front of me with a tiny baby wrapped in a blanket. Chris told me that she had just given birth at a hospital and was now returning home.

On the road, I drifted into and out of sleep. We stopped at places that looked as if there was nothing but forest, despite the people climbing on and off. The bus radio played American country songs. When the main road ended, we turned onto narrower muddier roads, and tree branches sometimes crashed into the windows.

Eventually we climbed off and got into the back of a rusted Toyota pickup with about twenty dark-faced passengers. I sat on the side rail next to an old man with oily hair and mirrored glasses and a young muscle-bound kid in a white tank top. We drove exceedingly fast through heavily forested hills and then flatlands where cattle roamed. When I asked how far it was to the jungle, Chris said only, "It's a ways still." This was just countryside. The truck bottomed out at least ten times, its carriage scraping dirt and rocks. Five hours later, after multiple military stops, my hair caked with dust, my hands burning from holding on to the rail, the truck stopped and the driver said we'd reached the end of the line. It was time to start walking.

We weren't anywhere I could locate on the map that Chris spread out on the grass. Even when he pulled out his GPS, we seemed to be standing in an unidentified span of green. As far as we could tell, we were about twelve miles north of the Río Blanco, but there was no road from here to there. Hills and forest lay in between.

It was midafternoon, the sun severe. Eventually Pancho found a trail that he felt would lead us to the river—or close to it. It was narrow and muddied by a morning rain. As we made our way forward, the cicadas blared in stereo, so loud, in fact, at times that the noise unbalanced me. I adjusted the straps on my sixty-pound backpack, though that didn't make it feel any lighter, and for a second I wondered if I had left anything else behind besides the snake gaiters. When I bent down to insert my soccer shin guards into the fronts and backs of my pants, Chris said, "Not now. The snakes will come later."

Pancho wore the same blue shirt that he had worn when we met three days before—and it still looked as if it had just been ironed. As he walked, he swung his machete at the brush and listened to his battery-powered radio for updates on the case of exiled president Mel Zelaya. At one point, he announced, "He's coming over the mountains on horseback." We never saw him.

Angel had changed from his dress shoes into black rubber farm boots that rose almost to his knees. Although he knew that there was no cellular coverage out here, every half hour or so he would extract his phone from his pocket, hold it up in the buggy air, and turn it on, at which point I would hear the Nokia's power-up jingle. Waving the phone, he would wait and wait for it to receive a signal—to no avail.

In time, the jingles of the Nokia powering up and down became a kind of joke among all of us; Angel seemed to think only about calling his girlfriends. "He's on the hunt," Pancho said. Laughing, Pancho made the sign for a telescope, as if he were sighting a woman miles away, through the thicket of green. Angel smiled, because he knew it was true.

Our pace was slow at first because of the brutal heat, which was closing in on 100 degrees, and the weight of our things. There were fields with cattle, then heavy jungle, then steep hills. Here and there I noticed big droopy plants like the potted ones sold at the plant stores in Brooklyn. For hours there was no one else in sight and no signs of habitation. My feet were comfortable in my combat boots, though I couldn't stop thinking that we were going the wrong way.

After a couple hours, I had to stop. We found a few boulders in a circle of shade and plunked down to eat Clif Bars. Resting there, my entire body began to throb, violently pulsing as if it might all just explode apart—my feet, my ankles, my legs, my chest, my shoulders, my back, my hands, even my eyes and the short strands of my sweaty hair.

When I looked up, I saw that Angel had taken off his boots and was massaging his bare feet. "By the end of this trip my feet are going to be raw," he said with a sour face.

That admission made me feel a little better. I got the impression that Pancho hadn't been completely open with him about the extent of our journey. "Did your father tell you we'd be walking every day?" I asked.

He shook his head, and Pancho smiled. "He told me there would a lot of walking," Angel said. "But not with this." He pointed at the backpack.

Suddenly Pancho put his hand in the air, as if he was demanding silence from the noisy insect world. He sensed things that the rest of us did not—or at least not immediately. He pointed at the path behind us. We all turned around, our attention rapt. As if materializing from the heat, a young woman appeared in thin-soled black flip-flops. She couldn't have been more than sixteen. She was pretty—slender, with long shiny black hair and a shy smile. She carried a young girl, no more than two years old, in one arm and a live blotchy white chicken in the other. The chicken had seen better days; it was missing feathers, and its beak was chipped. We stopped the girl, and I asked what she was doing out here and how far she'd walked. Angel was grinning, always happy to be around a girl.

She spoke to us in Spanish, saying that her name was Lucía and that she had already walked three miles. She said this casually, as if she'd just been out for a stroll down a paved suburban road. "Carrying your daughter like that?" I asked, incredulous. I couldn't imagine carrying my daughter in this heat, up and down these hills, let alone picking up my backpack again.

Lucía told us she was heading to her uncle's house, another two miles off, where she was going to deliver the chicken as a gift. She told us that some "loco" men had gunned down her twenty-one-year-old cousin a few hours earlier, during the night. He'd apparently been involved in a dispute over some nearby land. With very little evident emotion, as if reciting the weather, she said we'd see the blood in the path up ahead.

▾ ▾ ▾

IT WAS LONG after dark when we made it to the house of Alberto Aguilera. At first, we weren't sure whether we could trust him. Hours before, armed men on horseback had warned us that we couldn't stay just anywhere in the jungle. Big landholders were protective of their land. We wouldn't be safe sleeping outside until we entered the state reserve, which was still many days away. The riders suggested that we go to the third house; the owners of the others, they said, were "untrustworthy." But we hadn't seen any huts for miles. The sun had gone down, and even with our headlamps the dark was like a shut-up basement. We were too tired to go on, so we decided to take a chance.

We passed through an iron gate ringed with barbed wire and held our machetes at our sides. Several big dogs jumped out of the shadows, and a man yelled. As he approached us, I saw that he was shirtless, with a big hairy belly and a wide-brimmed brown cowboy hat. A handgun was tucked into his faded jeans. I heard pigs snorting somewhere in the dark.

Pancho stepped forward and explained to the man why we were out there. Alberto shook his head and smiled, and Pancho laughed. Pancho knew how to charm. When he came back to us, he said that Alberto was a good guy. We gave him rice and beans and a few packets of Tang, and he agreed to let us stay on the open porch of his two-room wood hut that night.

Alberto hung around with us as we rested on the dirt floor and ate rice that his wife had cooked earlier in the night. His wife was now asleep, and one of his boys sat next to him. There was no electricity, just a couple of candles flickering. Chris mused that the family was the modern-day equivalent of the nineteenth-century American "49ers" who had headed west for free or cheap land where they could forge a new life. He was no different from Pancho before violence forced Pancho out of the jungle.

Alberto had bushwhacked a path over the years to this hut and then populated his land with cattle. He owned a twenty-year-old modified 4×4 pickup, which he had parked a couple miles back along the path. Alberto had two brothers living a mile or so east. His village was called Perlas. Translated into English, *perlas* means "beads"—like a bead of sky cut out of the bush.

Never in my life hungrier, I ate four portions of rice. Night drew on, and I changed into dry clothes. When I peeled off my boots and socks, I saw that my left heel was one giant red blister. I tried to clean off my muddy boots with a wad of toilet paper that I had taken from the hotel in Catacamas. But the paper crumpled up into a dirty little ball without cleaning or drying much of anything. I fretted over my poor feet.

We slept on the floor, and for a second I thought about white sheets and a plush mattress. Maybe room service and a good movie. Just a break. But then I stopped myself. Amy would have laughed.

Before sleeping, we asked Alberto about the lost city. He knew about it but had never gone looking for it. A long time before, someone had told him that a gang of vicious jaguars protected the city. "I know Río Blanco," he said, referring to the river where Burke had told Morde "no white men had gone before" and the Indians had started to express concern about spirits. "It's not far from here. I'll tell you the way."

"ALL HAD FADED
INTO THIN AIR"

EACH VENTURE INTO the woods starts with two prayers," Morde wrote during his stay at Camp Ulak. "One that we will see no snakes, the other that we will get a jaguar."

A third may have been to strike it rich. Morde, Brown, and Burke prospected for gold up and down the flooding creek when they weren't searching for clues to the city—mounds in the soil, stray artifacts, anything. They backtracked along the rivers that had brought them to Ulak and investigated others they'd never seen. They mapped the land, their route through the river system; they were far beyond the expeditions of Strong, Mitchell-Hedges, and Captain Murray.

They rarely left camp without a gun. The expedition was now tracking in territory patrolled by natural-born killers, "where the treacherous tangled growth creeps down to the very edges for streams and where dread malaria . . . and jungle beasts roam." The one afternoon Morde did venture out unarmed, he caught the glassy eyes of a snake peeking out at him from behind a boulder as he cut through a swath of brush only three feet away. He and the snake stared at each other, and Morde felt his heart stop. He could see the deadly snake's slender triangular head angling for a quick strike, the yellow diamonds sewed across its back—a fer-de-lance. He froze for several minutes that felt like hours. The snake must have been eight feet long, he thought while slowly backing away. He was amazed that the snake didn't strike. Instead, it watched him—four paces, six, and then it was gone. Back at camp, Brown told him he looked as if he'd just seen a ghost. Lying down on his cot, Morde had the sensation that he'd just barely escaped death. "It was as if a machine gun had been trained on me," he reflected later. "A finger had reached for the trigger, then suddenly, the machine gun and all had faded into thin air. Or so it seemed."

▼ ▼ ▼

IN ALL, THE explorers spent about a month at Ulak, settling into a rhythm of river prospecting and hunting for signs of the city in the jungle around them. In photographs of those weeks at the edge of the world, Morde comes to look ragged. His gabardine pants are snipped off at the knees, and his brown safari shirt, rolled to the elbow, is streaked with dirt and wrinkled. His hair is greasy and pushed back, unwashed for weeks, his jaw chiseled into a look of determination, legs skinny as a boy's, though corded with muscle and strapped into tall black boots.

Their supplies, though, had thinned. They ate beans and smoked the stems of tobacco leaves. Sometimes Burke surprised them with dishes from the jungle. One night, they ate two toucans, chucking the colored feathers away. "Good eating, being all dark meat," Morde wrote of the cuisine. "More highly flavored than most similar small jungle birds." They ate wari when they could run them down, an occasional fish, something they called a "guinea pig like animal," and other birds. Burke became quite adept at making yellowtail pie.

As May turned to June, the rain came daily. The rivers continued to climb; the creek in front of their camp was only about eight feet from them now, which was cause for concern. "This afternoon at about 4 o'clock, a regular cloud burst descended on camp and drenched about everything," Morde wrote on June 8. They were grateful for the smaller showers that rinsed off their dirty bodies and washed their even dirtier clothes. When the rain came in torrents, however, the grounds around them turned to a mush that swallowed their feet, and tiny rivers guttered through the earth. There was nothing to do but wait for it to stop, the way hostages wait to be freed. Yet the stress of the rainy season only focused their obsession on finding the ruins.

In the day, roars like those of lions startled them. They stopped and stared up at the spears of daylight shooting through the canopy of trees. Other noises came to seem vaguely human, as if the jungle were attempting conversation. White-faced monkeys regularly ganged up on the three men, pitching branches and fruit down on them.

Burke identified rare birds. One day, they encountered a bird that he called a "Margarita," which he claimed was sacred to the Aztecs, as well as to the local Pech, who believed that the species descended from a beautiful woman who had been exiled into the mountains by a spurned lover. Each wing looked like a rising sun—a blaze of yellow offset by brown and black wing tips.

In what seemed like a fit of sentimentality for the lives they had left behind, the men decided to keep it as a pet and built it a cage out of bamboo. They called it Pete and hoped that it would act as a kind of watchdog for the camp. The hairy beasts, thankfully, remained elusive. "We found no traces of the legendary half human great apes," Morde reported.

Much of the details of the expedition's search parties for the lost city out of Camp Ulak are missing or vaguely sketched in the journal. There were some days when either Burke and Brown took to the pages and mentioned Morde going off on treks alone, taking along only his rifle and walking stick. What he did out there is unclear. No one ever says.

Maybe there was another journal, where those details were recorded. There was the chance, of course, that Morde's evasiveness was only boredom, that he didn't actually have anything to report and didn't want to engage any darker thoughts swirling in his mind. Such as, did the lost city even exist? Although he never wrote about his doubts, Morde surely worried deep down that he might never find anything in this endless jungle. You could walk for days and see nothing but trees and vines and rain, until it all started blurring together. But how could he live with that possibility? How would he muster the energy to go on? And what would he tell the world when he returned to New York? That he had spent four months in the jungle and discovered nothing?

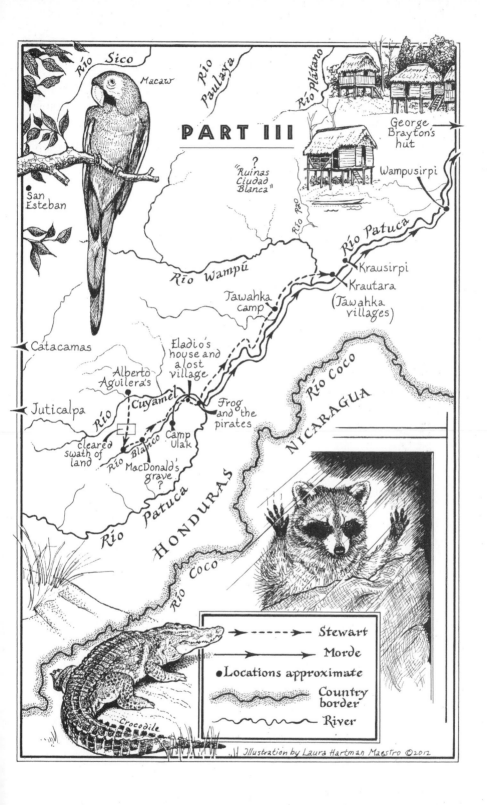

PART III

Río Sico

Macaw

Río Paulaya

Río Plátano

George Brayton's hut

"Ruinas Ciudad Blanca"

Wampusirpi

San Esteban

Río Paz

Río Patuca

Río Wampú

Krausirpi

Krautara (Tawahka villages)

Tawahka camp

Catacamas

Eladio's house and a lost village

Río Coco

Alberto Aguilera's

Juticalpa

Río Cuyamel

Frog and the pirates

NICARAGUA

cleared swath of land

Río Blanco

Camp Ulak

MacDonald's grave?

Río Patuca

HONDURAS

Río Coco

Crocodile

Stewart

Morde

• Locations approximate

Country border

River

Illustration by Laura Hartman Maestro ©2012

THE JUNGLE THAT DISAPPEARED

THIS IS WHERE Morde's world begins," Chris announced as we stumbled up a hillside. He flipped open his GPS and pointed over the lush valley. "Río Blanco should be over there."

"Should?" I asked.

"I could be wrong."

"And if you're wrong?"

"Then we should hope that we didn't walk too far away from where we have to go."

Pancho now took the lead, going off Alberto's directions to the river. It wasn't even nine o'clock, but we had already been walking for three hours and my feet were sore and soggy. Rain squalls blew up and vanished minutes later, leaving behind fizzing soil and blasting sun. The effects of Alberto's ten-sugar coffee had long worn off, and I was tired after a sleepless night on the ground, where I couldn't shake the thought that the snorting pigs around the hut might eat us. We had cut a curve through hillsides and over landscapes thick with creeping bushes and trees, ledges and drop-offs that gave way to flat swamplands swathed in high grass and fields where cattle milled beside clouds of mosquitoes.

Both my feet now had blisters, which had ripped open and turned into a pulp of purple and black, forcing me to walk on the front of my feet to reduce the pressure. At one point, Angel stopped to watch me limp by and snickered.

We passed small huts and saw men and women sitting on tiny porches or working patches of the cut jungle, and I wondered what they thought of our crew, outfitted with our combat boots, rip-resistant pants, quick-dry shirts, and giant backpacks. Some didn't seem to notice, while others watched us closely, observing the white dudes trekking through the jungle.

Soon there was no one but cattle and cut-down trees, dozens and dozens of blackened stumps in a wide-open space the size of probably six football fields. I was stunned and a little terrified. The impenetrable, supernatural-seeming mass of green that I had imagined had been completely and utterly slashed and burned. "So this is the jungle," I said sarcastically. It didn't exactly feel like Morde's dense malarial wilderness.

"It used to be," said Chris. "It was different in Morde's day."

Now the area looked like a giant lawn of ashes. Settlers, loggers, and ranchers had been clearing the jungle for years, illegally in many cases. "This is the colonization front," Chris said. Jungle clearing was a problem all over Honduras. The colonizers took the land for houses or pasture, or just for the wood. Many times they didn't replant anything.

In the last decade, the country had lost about 7 million acres (about 10,000 square miles) of forestland—an area the size of the combined Hawaiian Islands. Some of the timber ended up in products sold in the United States. The U.S. embassy has reported that the clearing continues at a rate of about 3 percent a year, further shrinking Central America's largest rain forest and everything—birds, beasts, bugs, and all manner of flora that double as herbal medicine for the local people—within.

As I traveled deeper into the jungle, I heard stories of bustling timber hubs hidden from the view of passing planes. Pancho told me about secret jungle trails wide enough for tractor-trailers to pass into and out of the deeper parts of the bush, clandestine sawmills and their shadowy overlords, or *chemiseros*. Sometimes the timber smugglers and even the ranchers worked with the narcos, who flew small planes into hacked-out landing strips. The absence of law enforcement contributed to the mayhem. Violence was always percolating. When the police did venture in, they were sometimes on the wrong side; they became protectors of the underworld, even hit men.

In 2006, a timber gang executed an environmentalist in the ragged mountains that climbed above the Río Patuca. He had been mapping the boundaries of a forest preserve near Olancho. The assassin was never found. A year later, to keep the family quiet, the gang returned in masks and murdered the dead man's brother, who was the sole witness, as well as his father-in-law and mother-in-law, who'd happened to be with him when the Mafia arrived to settle its score. No one was ever arrested.

That same year, around the same area, two more environmentalists were killed. That time, four policemen thought to be working with *chemiseros* did the work. They pulled the two men over as they traveled by car from Gualaco to Silca. I'd driven on the same forlorn dirt road on my way to Catacamas. Maybe the men thought at first that it was just a security stop. Maybe they thought, hey, it's no big deal, it's just the police. But they also might have known that they were in trouble. They were part of a prominent NGO called Environmental Movement of Olancho (MAO), and, like others who lobbied to save the diminishing jungle, they had been warned to stop bothering the loggers. Don't protest. Don't talk to the media. Keep your mouth shut, or else. But they hadn't listened. It was the life they had chosen. It was their land. The police told the men to get out of the car. One was forty-nine, the other twenty-nine. I heard the story at least three times. The police marched them to the center of the nearby town of Guarizama and stood them in front of a municipal building, as if to make a point to anyone who needed a lesson. You see this? Never cross us. We own this place. Some forty shots rang out, and the two bodies slumped to the ground.

Meanwhile, Pancho pointed at dark clouds piling up in the sky.

There was no time to dwell on the burned land. He turned and began to walk. "Are you sure we're going the right way?" I asked. Pancho didn't look back, which I took to be his way of saying that he was in control and we had already wasted enough of the day there.

It was almost noon when we spotted the Río Blanco, just as Alberto had said. From a high cliff, the river below stretched out like a gray scribble. We hurried down as the rain came, stumbling over rocks and vines, and came across a thatched hut. Pancho flipped off his cowboy hat and asked the old man inside for directions. Nodding, he invited us to sit on a wood bench. He said he knew the way to Ulak but warned us not to go.

"BEYOND HOPE"

WITHOUT EVIDENCE OF the ancient city, Morde turned again to rumor. The first story of Ciudad Blanca came from a man named Timoteo Rosales. When he encountered Rosales, however, is unknown; no date was recorded in Morde's journals. What is known is that Rosales worked as a rubber cutter, spending weeks wandering around the unmapped parts of the region, extracting from tree trunks the gummy white fluid known as latex. That fluid, after Rosales humped it to a river, was later turned into chewing gum and tires, among other things. He told Morde that it was in 1905, during a trek from the Río Paulaya to the Río Plátano—in the middle of the forest, far from any settlements—he looked up and saw stone "columns." He believed it was the lost city, though he hadn't stopped to linger over it. At another point in his travels, Morde met a man who claimed to have stumbled upon the ruins in 1898, at the place where the heads of the Plátano, Paulaya, and Wampú rivers come together. The man called the ruins "the White City"—the first and only mention of the name in Morde's logbooks. That was a big clue, but the area at the river heads covered more than a hundred square miles. They needed more to go on.

In time, they did discover traces of the ancient people who had dwelled there. From under dirt and rocks, they dug up six stone flutes, numerous razor blades, and stone household items such as pots, spoons, and grinding slabs. They also uncovered tiny religious idols, with faces contorted by weather and time, and small masks resembling monkey faces. All of it made them wonder: could the people who made these things have inhabited the lost city?

Most amazingly, they encountered earth-covered mounds, rising like small, toppled buildings. Indians they met described the ancient people who lived in these deep parts as master stone builders. Because of this, Morde wrote of the city, "the [Indians] insisted, much had been preserved." He also heard about a long-staired approach to the center, paved in bleached stones and flanked by "larger than life statues of frogs, crocodiles and monkeys."

The dramatic description echoed other outlandish accounts of lost cities. In his search for El Dorado in 1542, the conquistador Francisco de Orellana wrote of "one town that stretched for 15 miles without any space from house to house," and he observed "many roads here that entered into the interior of the land, very fine highways." He recalled too "very large cities that glistened in white." .

The most shocking thing Morde heard during those weeks was a detail of the White City's center. "At the heart of the place was a temple," an Indian told him, "with a high stone platform on top of which rose the towering the statue of the Monkey God himself."

The city might be around any bend, over any hill. But as Morde and the others drew closer, the jungle seemed to grow more aggressive in its efforts to thwart their mission. "We have met our match in the jungle," he wrote. One day, rain blew the roof off the camp's sleeping hut; snakes and termites invaded; the water continued to rise, threatening to flood the living quarters and muddying the creek waters, making any further prospecting impossible; the dam broke once and for all. It was, as the Spanish put it, the *chubasco*, the squall. "The rain is incessant," Morde went on. "Tempers are easily ruffled, the camp is damp and messy and the creek is beyond hope." Another time, he added, "We often think . . . how infinitesimal we three white men are here in the green vastness."

On June 11, they woke to Pete the bird's frantic chattering. When they stepped outside to see what it was all about, they noticed the tracks of an adult jaguar. It had circled the camp, emerging from the depths of the jungle as if to mark its territory.

Burke, Brown, and Morde peered at the perimeter of their camp, where they heard voices. The brush disgorged five men. Four were Indians, and the fifth was a white man who introduced himself as William A. MacDonald. MacDonald was from San Francisco but worked as a mining scout for a Toronto company. By his looks, he was middle-aged. When he spoke, his voice was so soft that the buzzing jungle made it hard for the explorers to hear him. Mac-Donald said he'd been paddling upriver for three weeks and was now camped out on the Blanco, a few miles back. He asked about their prospecting.

Who is this man? Morde wondered. Was he also searching for the lost city? Would he try to steal from them? "He caused us great queasiness by his question of gold," Morde wrote. Terror seized them. They steered the conversation away from their own activities in the jungle and pressed MacDonald for news of the war. The Americans, MacDonald said, were getting closer to entering the battle, which made the explorers only more uneasy about the world that awaited them upon their return to New York.

MacDonald and his men stayed for three hours before a rainstorm hit and they fled, worrying that the creek was about to flood. Even then, the encounter lingered with Morde and Brown. They felt suspicious of the scout, and they resolved to move out. "The best course is to wind down our affairs here, as hastily as possibly," Morde wrote. "We will be able to get a line on MacDonald from our friends on the Patuca, who will possibly be able to give us some hint as to his plans." They couldn't risk MacDonald following them. Decamping was the only way to protect what they already knew.

LOOKING FOR CAMP ULAK

THERE'S A WOMAN who lives up there," the old man said to us in Spanish. "She's a witch. We call her La Sucia." The dirty woman.

The man wore dusty black sandals, ragged shorts, and a white T-shirt. He was probably in his eighties. His fingers were grimy, and his hands coarse and callused. The Río Blanco roared from behind his hut. I noticed insects sneaking in through cracks in the damp walls—millipedes, fat shiny flies. Ants made their way in a vein across the smooth dirt floor, vanishing under the raised board that served, with a couple of neatly folded blankets on top, as his bed.

He told us that he had prospected the region's rivers for decades. He had found some gold but not enough to make him rich. About thirty years ago, he had decided to move here from Catacamas and build a hut, a few miles up the Blanco. Now about half a dozen other mud huts dotted a grassy path. But even though they'd created this place here, if the village decided to leave one day, it would not be very long before everything would simply melt away into the surrounding greenery. The man called his hut "far away from things," and the slow, quiet way he talked, along with the rain coming down, imbued his words with the mysticism of fairy tales.

"The witch protects the gold at Ulak," he said. "There is gold there, and when men go, they see her." He paused and opened his eyes very wide, as if imagining the sight. "She is a pretty woman with black hair. You might see her washing her clothes in the creek."

I asked if he had seen her. He clucked as though that was a stupid question.

"The men who see her don't leave," he said.

I knew that this was only a legend, just as the monkey men were merely legends, though he seemed very serious about the story. Later, I would find out that it was a common story throughout Central America. The witch was called dirty because she never left the forest. She used her beauty to lure men into her hideout. Sometimes she sang, and her voice sounded like a waterfall or a mountain breeze, depending on who told the story. I almost laughed it away until the old man mentioned the dead American.

"It was a long, long time ago," he said. "The gringo was looking for gold around Ulak. And then he got a fever."

I told him the story of Morde, hoping to stir some distant memory, but he didn't know the name. I mentioned the San Francisco miner MacDonald, who had traveled up this way almost seventy years before. I knew it was a long time ago, but I wondered if the dead man he was talking about might be MacDonald. In Morde's notes, there is no further mention of the miner. He didn't see him on the Río Blanco as he left Ulak, and he heard nothing about him from the Indians or the Germans on the Patuca. It seemed as though he had evaporated.

The old settler contemplated what I told him. He said that sometimes he found "ancient things" in the ground in the forest—broken pottery and stone slabs. But he knew of no ruins around there. He had heard of men looking for them but didn't know if MacDonald was the dead man. It was just a story. "You can go to his grave. You'll see it. He's buried near Ulak in a shade of trees."

Pancho asked the settler where to find a mule to haul our things for a bit, and soon a young man from the settlement appeared. He had a rifle slung over one shoulder. His hair stuck up in every direction, and his smile, under a wisp of a mustache, revealed a set of blackened teeth. The rain had ceased, and the sun was back. We threw our things onto his animal, which was already huffing in the heat, and the man pointed at the shin guards fastened to my legs. He mumbled something that I didn't understand. Chris interpreted: "He wants to know if you're playing in a soccer game out here."

▼ ▼ ▼

FOR A FEW hours, we made our way along the twisting Río Blanco toward Morde's camp. I complained about my blistered feet, but no one seemed to care. The Blanco was a fast-flowing river, about fifty yards across in some stretches. The heat got worse as the day sank into late afternoon. It rose in waves off the high grass, which I watched for snakes. At one point, Pancho bent over and picked something out of the grass. ".357," he said, holding in the cup of his hand an empty bullet casing that didn't look very old. He scanned the mostly flat landscape around us, blurry with sun, but there was no one else in sight.

My mind wandered a lot as we walked through these boring stretches of flatness. A million totally random thoughts rattled around inside my head like a pop song that was impossible to shake.

Sky does such a good cannonball; What's that line from T. S. Eliot about the return of a journey is the beginning?; Man, I'd love a cheeseburger—with relish!; She's going to be in preschool; Where did all that time go? Where will we end up?; That biker actually died; I can't do this; Snakes!; Amy's right; She's got a journey too; Where are we?; You're a complete idiot; What's that line?; You return to the place you started and know it for the first time.

After a couple more hours, I realized that Chris had dropped behind us. By now we had probably walked eight or nine miles and had come upon some formidable hills. I waited for him to catch up and saw that his face had gone pale. "Something bit me," he said, shaking his head. He pulled off his glasses and wiped the sweat from his forehead. "I'm burning up with a fever. I'm freezing." His blue shirt was drenched in sweat.

"Should we stop?" I asked.

"We gotta keep going," he said. "Night's coming." He wanted to make it to Ulak. Then he would rest.

I worried selfishly that we'd have to turn around and get him to a hospital, which would mean days of backtracking. It was hard for me even to imagine the energy it would take to walk back to Catacamas.

We slipped down a cliff face and traversed the Blanco on a narrow mahogany pitpan that was lying abandoned on the mucky shore. As we crossed, Chris said, "Morde probably prospected for gold here. We can't be far from his camp." I could tell he was struggling by the slow and labored manner of his speech and the way he kept staring off into the buzzing morass, probably dreaming of being somewhere else. That was not the film that he wanted his wife to be watching.

On the other side, the mule guide declared, "It's up here."

We followed him up the hill and into some of the densest foliage we had yet encountered. Trees rose high around us, eclipsing the sun. Pancho stopped and pointed at the ground. "He's buried somewhere here," he said. "The gringo."

There was a mossy rock the size of a small headstone embedded in the jungle floor, and I pictured the bones of the dead man buried beneath.

"What if that's MacDonald?" I asked.

No one responded. The hissing green was loud in my head. An unexpected sadness came over me. Here was a man who had come to Honduras with dreams of striking it rich. He had left behind a small world to chase the potential of a bigger one. His quest had ended badly, and he had never made it home. Did he have a wife or children? Did anyone back home ever learn that he died? Or did they think he'd just run away?

The man's story reminded me of Evelyn Waugh's blackly comic novel *A Handful of Dust*. The hero, Tony Last, gets lost in the Amazon on an expedition looking for El Dorado, only to be imprisoned by a crazy man who, unknown to anyone, forces him to read Charles Dickens out loud for the rest of his life. Whatever the circumstances of the dead man's disappearance, he was here and no one knew about him, except for the old settler along the river—and now me.

I got a bad feeling in my head. I hoped at that second that Amy and Sky didn't think that I was running away from them. I recalled the time not long before when Sky had actually asked why I went away so much. "Why do you always leave us?" The question had stunned me at first. I thought for a second and then told her that it was my job to go away. But that hadn't satisfied her. "So why don't you get another job, Daddy?"

Amy and I had debated my freelance life incessantly, particularly how there was nothing steady about it: paychecks were erratic, health insurance was nonexistent, overseas trips came up at the last minute. The conversations, which happened mostly late at night, sometimes after a couple drinks or while we were lying in bed with the lights out, had been minimal when it was just Amy and me, but they had grown after we'd had Sky and bought a place.

It wasn't that Amy wanted our family to be like everyone else's family, just that we make a home that had some consistency, some predictability to it. Part of me understood that, but the other part— the part that enjoyed the romance of being out in the world—kept thinking that I would wait just another year before making some changes.

Sky, however, had her own ideas. One afternoon, as we walked past the local firehouse, she said, "You should be a fireman, Daddy. Then you wouldn't need to go anywhere." I smiled, because I loved how she could make sense of a world that was so complicated to me.

Chris was too sick to care. "I have to get into the water," he said abruptly. The mule guide attempted to intervene.

"Don't get in the river. There are crocodiles."

Chris shook his head. "I'll be fine."

"There are big crocodiles. They eat people here."

But Chris wasn't hearing any of it. He didn't even bother taking off his clothes or his combat boots. He looked at me through his glasses, blinked, and then stepped through a hole in the verdure, which dropped down a steep hill that fell away into the river.

For a moment I stared at the jungle that swallowed him, and then Pancho said we had to move on. Staggering forward, I caught glimpses of the rushing river but saw no sign of Chris, and I worried briefly that he would not make it back. I remembered Morde describing the beady red eyes of dozens of crocodiles lurking on the riverbanks. I felt guilty for being more concerned about my trip than about Chris's sickness. Rain came and went, and the strange green noises played with my head.

Half an hour passed before we stumbled down a rock face to the river edge and there he was—drenched, his shirt and pants sticking to him, his wire-rimmed glasses fogged up. "I made it!" he yelled over the noise of the river. The color in his face had been mostly restored. His voice was strong. Seeing him soaking there, I thought, This is why his students call him Indiana Jones. He was a little out of his mind. "Ahhh," he said, dripping. "That was great!" Then his eyes widened a bit more and he pointed at a narrow creek emerging from the wilderness. "That must be Ulak."

▼ ▼ ▼

THIS WAS WHERE, Morde had said, "no white man has been before." But there didn't seem to be anything left of his camp. Trees and brush had reclaimed the area where the three huts had likely once stood. Vines dangled over the mossy green waters of the Ulak, which stretched about thirty feet across. I stared for a moment at the overgrown creekside, trying to envision Morde on the site almost seventy years before—his daily comings and goings in his cutoff pants, the makeshift wood table he constructed to compose his journals, the talk of the lost city at night as Burke or Brown played harmonica, and later MacDonald emerging from the brush to the queasy astonishment of the explorers. But I couldn't see any of it. The jungle had obliterated him and the entire scene.

"This way," said Chris. "Let's see if we can find anything else."

The strong rapids fought us as we stumbled through the waist-deep water. On the other side of the creek, we used our machetes to hack up a hill that Morde had probably hacked through dozens of times when he went out hunting or to pee. Just as a squall hit, the leafage fell away and we stepped into a pasture of chest-high grass, where a lone hut of wood and thatch stood. Farther off three emaciated cows grazed. It wasn't more than a two-minute walk from the creek. At least five acres of trees had been cleared, all jungle when Morde was there.

We went to the hut and found two women stirring a tub of cau-jada, a local cheese, made of curdled milk boiled for hours and fruit juices. The women wore loose dresses and looked frightened at our sudden presence. They couldn't have been older than twenty, with long black hair knotted down their backs. The hut was only a single room with floors of raked dirt. The thatched roof shifted in the rain as water dripped through cracks and made puddles on the floor. When I asked how long the girls had been here, they hesitated before saying, "About a year." What they were doing there, though, they didn't say. I got the feeling that before our coming they had had other encounters with less friendly sorts and were anxious about what we were up to.

We said good-bye, spent an hour walking around the pasture, and made one long sweep of the Ulak. We didn't see the hairy men or discover any evidence of Morde's visit. "It's gone. There's nothing here," Chris said. "We should go."

The Tawahkas were two or three days' travel by river, the last living connection to Morde's expedition and the lost White City. Only they would know where to go.

"NO TRACE OF RUINS"

WE FOUND DANGER at almost every bend," Morde wrote as the expedition raced downstream to the Tawahka outpost, eager to move on and to defend against the snooping MacDonald, if necessary. The dugout canoe shot through the Río Blanco and then the Cuyamel. In places, the current surged to twelve miles per hour, sending up thrashing armies of waves. Brown was at the stern while Burke steered at the bow and looked for smoother channels. Morde worked an eight-foot wooden pole at the center and bailed out incoming water. "If any of us were thrown into the river, we wouldn't have a chance," he worried. "Knife-like rocks would rip our bodies apart."

They had Pete the bird with them, and he cried all day, as if warning the explorers of something they had overlooked. It was June 15, almost three months from the day they had arrived in the country. With their heavy, knotted beards, Morde, Burke, and Brown looked like primitive men. Their clothes were ratty and hung loose on their rail-thin frames. Their boots were junk. Morde wrote of the bugs that attacked their bodies. Deer flies swarmed the muggy air, and sand flies "by the millions came . . . and ate us alive."

The force of the river kept growing with every turn. One stretch of the Cuyamel that had taken eight hours to navigate upstream took forty-eight minutes down. They shot over a five-foot precipice and at another turn smashed into a rock, nearly splitting the boat in half, then tumbled over another small waterfall.

In placid spots the men caught their breath and took in a passing landscape that they no longer fully recognized. They had traveled these waters for almost a month now, and the last few days of rain had transformed the riverbanks. Sandbars were gone. Tall trees had been swept away. The churning river had turned from murky green to the frothy light brown of overcreamed coffee. The men had worried that the river would eventually turn on them and now it had.

"As we swept around curves, the cat-claw and thorns snatched at us. Many times we lay supine in the bottom of the pitpan as the current ahead sent us under the hungry vines," Morde wrote like a soldier who was suddenly on a fast retreat. "Our landmarks were gone," he continued. "Monkeys howled and barked at our passage." He knew there was not much time left for them before the rains rendered the jungle unnavigable.

They aimed to make the Patuca by nightfall but fell short. "We decided to gamble and push on," Morde wrote toward the middle of the afternoon that day. "But as always, we lost. The skies darkened and opened up." The storm forced them to land the boat. Soaking wet, they cut away enough vegetation for a place to lie down and raised a protective roof of waja leaves. Through the wet night they huddled there, waiting out the squall and trying to recoup their energy. "Minutes dragged like hours, as the night wore on," Morde wrote. "We smoked, talked twisted and scratched and stayed awake. Sleep was impossible. . . . Our feet stuck out in the rain."

The next morning the light was dim. The men ate crackers that tasted of the flies that had been buzzing around them the day before. The specter of the miner MacDonald lingered in their daydreams. They reached the Patuca, which was running as fast as the Cuyamel. Morde's shoulders throbbed from working the pole. His body was bruised and scratched. Mosquitoes had drawn blood. The last day and a half of river travel felt like the last stage of a very long battle.

When they finally emerged from the rapids, Brown fell sick. His body convulsed with chills, and Morde wrapped him in blankets and took his spot at the stern. There was concern that the expedition was coming apart. After a few more hours on the river, they finally arrived at the Tawahkas' settlement. But they were too tired to talk. "We didn't bother to eat. We set up cots and slept."

When Morde awoke the next morning, he had a conversation with the tribal elder about the lost city. The two men had apparently become friends; Morde, it seemed, had turned the chief into a kind of informant. "Nicolas stated positively there was no trace of ruins up the Wampu," he wrote. "We are convinced no great civilization ever existed up there and that there are no archaeological discoveries of importance to be made."

CALLING HOME

How much farther?" I asked Chris.

He kept swinging his machete at the lush green in front of him, ignoring me because I had asked the question half a dozen times already.

The Tawahka camp was at least thirty more miles away, with no direct route, and we had been walking with the mule guide for five hours straight, without resting more than fifteen minutes for a Clif Bar. I tried to think of anything but of the next step forward and the pain it would cause. Our goal seemed so far. Thirty miles? That was like walking from Brooklyn out to Westchester.

"Maybe we should just stop here for the night," I suggested, pointing at a conveniently located cut in the forest that looked as though it had been created for us.

"You sound like my kids," Chris said finally.

"But I'm not gonna make it."

"Stop thinking about it and you will."

I couldn't believe Chris was even standing up after his river dunking. He still looked a little pale, and I could hear him breathing harder on the hills. I told him it would help me to know about how much farther we had to go.

"You really want to know?"

I said I did.

"I don't know."

I tried to jot down notes when it wasn't raining, but the vicious mud kept grabbing my boots and putting unbearable pressure on my blisters, and I couldn't gather enough strength to stop and write. Because of the heat, I drank about three or four gallons of water a day, but the sun sucked almost all of it out of me.

The forest grew denser, and our progress slowed. At one point it took an hour just to hack through the length of a football field, and then we hit a cliff face and were forced to turn around. On two occasions, military helicopters swooped by overhead, searching for something that wasn't there. What were we searching for? At times I forgot.

At the Río Cuyamel, which ran wider and swifter than the Blanco, with an electric green color that in places resembled Palmolive dish soap, we glanced up and saw a dark wall of mountains towering over us like the prow of an incoming freighter ship. Pancho warned against crossing the mountains, swinging his machete at the fog-encased peaks. "It could take us two or three days to get to the other side."

Chris and Pancho discussed building a raft out of balsa trees, but our mule guide said that the strong rapids would destroy a make-shift boat within the first mile. He made a gesture with his hands of snapping wood. I wanted to float down the river, even if it meant on a stick of wood—anything not to walk another step. I closed my eyes, stood still in the late-July sun, and felt the jungle pressing in on my hurting body, toying with my thoughts. Its rains and rivers and beasts of prey, the endless shadows. When I opened my eyes, Pancho called out from ahead that he saw a house on a hill above the river. Maybe, I thought, the people there could help get us out.

▼ ▼ ▼

A MIDDLE-AGED MAN named Eladio lived there with his wife and two young girls. At first he was a bit skeptical of our group. "*Gringos?*" he said. "*Americano?*"

Chris told him in Spanish that we were from the United States, even though we looked as though we'd just climbed out of a beaver hole—hair matted down and greasy, clothes a muddy mess, Chris's face looking pale again from the tropical sickness. The two girls whispered and laughed. Eladio bit his lip. "Are you military?" He pointed at Chris's and my combat boots. "Those look like they're army."

The man was short and muscular and wore an unbuttoned white short-sleeve dress shirt and pleather sandals. "The American army used to be out here," he said. He made a capacious gesture at the sky, as though he were describing a gigantic bird. "They would come in big helicopters that you could hear from far away."

He was referring to the U.S. soldiers who in the 1980s had secretly trained the rebel contras to wage war in socialist-held Nicaragua across the border. Nicaragua was an eight- or nine-hour walk from here.

"It was a scary time," Eladio said. "At night we would all go to bed early and blow out all the candles because we didn't want anyone to notice us here. You never knew who was coming through that jungle." He paused. "I knew the Americans were out there, but I didn't see them. They were ghosts."

In his polite southern way, Chris said, "We're not in the army." He explained that we were trying to get to the Tawahkas on the Patuca.

The man relaxed and smiled. He said he hadn't seen any boats in days except for a makeshift timber barge that had motored by that morning. When Chris asked if it might be back, Eladio made a face as if he'd just swallowed a bug. It would likely be back, but its people couldn't be trusted. While we figured out what to do, Eladio said we could stay the night, but not in his house. He gestured at the small open porch, which was really just an extension of the hill dropping off into the river below.

We used the last bits of the afternoon to sharpen our machetes and get some rest. Later, Chris woke me from a nap on the porch. "You gotta see this." He waved me to the back side of the hut, just past the outhouse, and into a small pasture, where a tall, grassy bump rose about fifteen feet high. "You know what this is?" he asked.

He looked excited despite the tropical sickness. "A hill," I said, a bit mockingly, thinking that, like me, he needed some sleep.

"It's a lost city."

"What?"

"Well, it's not a lost city exactly, but it's a lost village."

As I digested this notion, he went on. "This is the plaza," he said, walking over the bump. "And those smaller mounds are houses," he said, indicating rises in the earth about twenty yards off. "It was probably a village of about fifty people."

"How long ago?"

"It's hard to guess, but I'd say it's more than a thousand years old."

▼ ▼ ▼

THERE WAS NO sign of the timber pirates returning, and the river ran empty for the rest of the evening. But other concerns momentarily trumped our travel problems. Pancho's radio spoke of a civil war. It had been almost a month since the coup had begun, and the crisis was headed toward a climax. Airstrips were in military lockdown; there was a moratorium on travel throughout the country the next day; and Honduran troops were lining up at the Nicaraguan border, where the exiled president Mel Zelaya was promising to cross with a personal army. It was now illegal for stores to sell guns or ammunition, but people on both sides of the dispute were finding ways to arm themselves.

I could hear Pancho and Eladio only in bits over the cicadas.

"Chavez wants to bring communism here," Pancho said.

"Yes, Mel is risking that," Eladio admitted.

"And communism would ruin this country."

"But we would all be poor. I think that is good."

"But how would we make any money? You have to think about that."

"It doesn't matter as much to me, making money—but the

millionaires will lose all their money. That's what matters. That they are poor like us."

Pancho cracked a smile. "Maybe that's something good," he replied. "I just don't want a strongman telling us how to live. There are Castro and Chávez and Ortega. And those people there are poor and live under a strongman. No one wants another strongman here. It is good to be free." To that, they agreed.

The radio played on, and Eladio looked at me and said, "You should go home."

▼ ▼ ▼

WE WENT TO sleep early after a tasty dinner of rice, beans, and freshly made tortillas that Eladio's wife prepared over a wood fire—what had become our daily diet. Chris had gone to bed hours before, feeling the return of his fever. It was about 8 p.m., and though it had been dark for little more than an hour it already felt like midnight.

Pancho helped me hang my hammock between two trees next to the house, tying the rope at each end into knots I'd never seen before. The only time I had ever been inside the hammock was back on my Brooklyn roof deck. When it's hanging, it looks a lot like a pod, the bottom side a green stretchy vinyl, which grabs hold of you, and the top side tightly netted with a zippered opening.

I spent some time reading by headlamp while mosquitoes attacked the netting around me. I hoped the trees wouldn't snap. I had changed into dry clothes, and even though I hadn't slept more than twelve hours over the last three days, I couldn't fall asleep. My feet were on fire. I imagined how quietly a jaguar might approach and what it would feel like to be attacked from below, all of a sudden. After an hour, I unzipped the hammock, grabbed the satellite phone from one of Chris's bags on the porch, and headed into the ruins behind the hut.

The mound shone a pale green. I could see more stars than I knew existed and the bluish peaks and valleys on the moon, which shone against the pure black of night like a flashlight. Three times I followed the flickering tail of a shooting star.

I hadn't used the phone until now because I had wanted to try to be as alone as possible and also because the technology seemed so incongruent to this place. But it was almost Sky's birthday, and I needed to hear my family's voices. Eventually I turned on the phone, pressed the numbers of my Brooklyn home, and then listened as the phone searched for a line. It rang three times before Amy picked up.

"Is that really you?" she asked.

She was two hours ahead of me and was cooking dinner. It was good to hear her voice.

I started to tell her about what was going on, but she cut me off. "We were attacked last night," she said.

I wasn't sure that I'd heard her right, so I asked her to say it again. "The phone is a little static-y," I said.

"I woke up in the middle of the night to an animal pulling off the screen," she said, her voice getting shaky. "It was trying to get in the house."

"What do you mean attacked?"

"It had these huge yellow eyes and hands. A raccoon," she said.

"A raccoon was trying to get into the house?"

I tried to make a joke about how it was me who was supposed to be talking about animal attacks, but she was really shaken up. She hated raccoons, was terrified of their black-masked eyes.

"It's serious," she said. "It had these huge ugly hands."

She said it had fled when she jumped out of bed, but the screen had been mostly peeled away. "I might have rabies," she said.

"How would you get rabies?"

"Maybe I got some of its saliva on me from the screen."

I tried to calm her down. But she was speeding forward. She said that after she had closed the window and locked it, she had washed her hands with Lysol.

"Lysol?"

"I was scared," she said. "I thought that would disinfect me."

"You don't have rabies," I said. "You're okay."

"But it could come back. It was huge. It could easily come back."

I told her that even if it did return it couldn't break through the glass.

"You didn't see these hands," she said. "They were huge. They could break glass."

We went back and forth about it before she said that she was now sleeping in Sky's room and kept all the lights on in the house.

"It's because you're away," she said finally. "I have to deal with this all by myself."

A moment passed, and silence filled the line. I felt a terrible sadness ripple over me. I wished I could teleport myself back there and track down that damn raccoon. I started to tell her how sorry I was, but just then Sky came on the line. "Daddy," she said. Her voice was a relief. It was so cheerful. I could see her on the other side, both of them sitting at the dining room table, Sky bouncing in her chair as she clutched the phone.

"How is the jungle?" she asked.

I told her it was hot and wet. Then we talked about the princess she'd drawn at camp and she wondered if I had seen any monkeys. "Do you wear socks in the jungle?" she asked. That made me laugh. Amy too.

"Are you excited for your birthday?" I asked.

She said, "Super, super excited," and ticked off the friends who planned to come to the party.

"That sounds amazing," I said.

We talked for a long time, the tension melting away. I told Sky, "Be good for Mommy, okay?" In the end, it was difficult to say good-bye. There is always more to say, of course. "I'm sorry that I'm not there," I said.

"I'm just tired," Amy answered before the line went dead.

Back in the hammock, I couldn't find a Valium, so I just closed my eyes. My head was warm, and I began to worry that I had contracted whatever Chris was fighting off. I felt as though something

inside was slowly coming undone. I thought about the raccoon ripping off the screen and imagined it as a metaphor for the shame I
had felt in leaving and in framing the quest as a hunt for myself. It
seemed like a kind of intruder trying to tear apart my family. How
selfish was I? I kept hearing Amy say, "I'm just tired," and worried
about her. Were there costs to this trip that I had ignored or mis-
read?

Before I'd left the city I hadn't actually considered what it would
mean to miss Sky's birthday. I'd thought I'd make it up to her when
I got home—she'd have one every year. But now I just felt sad and
detached. When I finally slept, it was a restless sleep, with a string
of weird malaria-medicine dreams, where soaring trees came to life
and the buried American kept telling me that I'd stolen his gold. In
the morning when I awoke, the pirates had already arrived.

"THE LOST CITY
OF THE MONKEY GOD"

JUST AS MORDE was about to give up on the expedition, he spied something from the top of a small cliff.

The men had hiked for hours, if not days, macheteing through a morass of vines and brambles as the summer rain poured down. They were tired, starving, fighting off sickness, and thinking of calling it quits. Going home, as all the others had done.

But then there it was, "plainly visible below, protruding from the jungle," as Morde wrote later in a cover story that appeared in the Hearst Sunday magazine the *American Weekly*.

What was Morde's first response?

Perhaps he closed his eyes and then slowly opened them again, just to make sure that what he was seeing was real: the crumbling walls of a city, some as tall as he was or taller, and hills like carpets that looked haphazardly thrown over things. Or maybe, feeling so overwhelmed, feeling so grateful at the sight of the ruins, he knelt down on the soggy ground, his tired and battered body pulsing, and kissed it, to feel the old wet earth and know that it was still under him. Or perhaps he simply stood there and looked, wanting to keep it all within his gaze so it wouldn't ever go away, so that he would always remember that moment.

Whatever he or Brown did, Morde never said.

Around them, the light was dim as a cellar, with only a few beams of sunlight splintering through. They probably had to squint. Water dripped from the high canopy. The site was blanketed in centuries of growth; mold, giant trees, and vines. It was easy to understand why the city had stayed concealed for so many decades. How would anyone have ever found it, unless by sheer chance?

They waded into the ruins. "With our machetes, we uncovered crude stone implements—broken pieces of ancient pottery and razor-like knives of volcanic glass." They turned up crumbled rocks with carvings that suggested outlines of monkeys. Further on, "we found . . . walls upon which the green of the jungle had worked small damages and which had resisted the flood of vegetation."

At least one embankment was twelve feet tall and about three feet wide—"a man-made stone wall, carefully set together stone on stone." There Morde imagined that an ancient wall had probably risen to at least thirty feet and functioned as a protective barrier against the city's enemies.

They followed the stone structures as far as possible, watching how they either disintegrated altogether or became engorged by grass and vines and disappeared under towering grassy mounds. The mounds, Morde believed, were old buildings covered up by jungle growth and by this measure evidence of once "great buildings," an especially astounding concept considering that the inhabitants had had only their bare hands to build with. Who were they? he kept wondering. Ghosts of this land.

As they took all of it in, branches cracked loudly overhead. "Monkey faces peered inquisitively at us from the surrounding screen of dense foliage," Morde wrote in the magazine article, as if they had been caught somewhere they were not supposed to be.

Farther on, he noticed adjoining ruins, suggesting that the city continued to unfold in all directions and for many acres. "There are indeed buildings beneath their age-old shroudings," he wrote excitedly.

Morde wrestled with the fact that although the ancient people had built their civilization out of stone, the nearby tribes of Tawahka and Pech had preferred mud and wood. Was there a direct line of descent? he mused. And if so, why had the custom of building changed? The riddle of the place only deepened, made him more anxious to understand it. But at the same time it enlivened him, lit him up. After the many boat trips, the miles of grueling jungle walks, the sleepless nights, the jaguars, everything, he had found it—the place that almost four hundred years before, the conquistadors had likely sought. This was his discovery.

▼ ▼ ▼

HE DUBBED IT "The Lost City of the Monkey God," not the White City, which was the name that had been used for centuries. For Morde, the new name reflected the lingering legend among the river tribes of the terrifying hairy men who inhabited the deepest parts of the forest. The name also seemed to suggest another motivation at play: it was sensational enough that people would take notice and, most important, remember.

▼ ▼ ▼

MORDE NEVER ACTUALLY noted the specific date of his finding, only that it had occurred at the very end of his journey, as the men were fleeing. He was also vague about the location of the ruins, perhaps influenced by the Heye Foundation's desire to keep any big find initially out of the public view. In his notebooks Morde recorded neither a latitude nor longitude—maybe because he didn't know them. But he did report opaquely that the site stood at the heads of the Paulaya and Plátano rivers, a nearly impassable area of hundreds of square miles in the eastern part of the country. "It was an ideal site for the city," he reported in the *American Weekly* story. "Towering mountains formed the backdrop of the scene."

That is where, perhaps, his expedition walking stick came in. On it, at some point, Morde carved out thirty-three sets of numbers and directional instructions—perhaps his route back to the city—down the four sides of the angled handle. Like any well-trained spy,

Morde made sure the stick numbers were notably ambiguous—offering no specific starting or end point—so as to prevent others from using them.

There was no time, however, for the men to learn much more about the ruins. The sky darkened, as it always did, and they were forced to move on. "The rainy season," Morde lamented, "put a stop to our labors." The rain bearing down on them ruled out any efforts at excavation. Plus, he added, "We had no equipment to continue digging deeper into the ruins." After a day or so of roaming the site, Morde wrote, with surprisingly little drama, that they had collected their things and left the lost city behind.

OUR TIME WITH THE PIRATES

THE PIRATE BOAT glided up to where we were standing on the muddy shore. It was a narrow forty-foot mahogany dugout, equipped with a forty-horsepower Yamaha engine. Three men were on board, one at the bow and two at the stern. They looked as if they'd just been through a bar fight: their clothes were in shreds and stuck to their rain-soaked bodies; the tallest had a jagged scar across his cheek. All were armed with pistols tucked into their waistbands, and one leaned on a machete. Stepping ashore, the oldest man, who seemed to be in charge, tipped his white sombrero and said, *"Hola!"*

He was short and muscular with a closely shaved goatee. He wore white jeans tucked into rubber boots and a white dress shirt open enough at the chest to reveal a rosary necklace. His watch was gold, and so were his teeth. He asked if we wanted to go downriver. He spat into the water. Chris looked at me as if to ask, what do you think? But there was no other way.

"Two hundred dollars," the leader grunted. Chris told him $50, but we settled on $75, passed over the cash, and climbed on.

I sat near the bowman with Chris and kept a machete at my feet; it was sharp enough to slice off a man's fingers. "We have to be vigilant," Chris whispered, looking up at the bowman, a toothless thug in a dragon-patterned tank top and military pants cut off at the knees. "These guys are some serious roughnecks."

Angel sat on a pile of supplies at the center. He didn't joke with his cell phone anymore or mention the girls he was hunting back home. The smile was gone. He stared out over the churning water with a troubled look. So did his father. The last time Pancho had gotten that look, we'd been driving through bandit country. I wondered if we'd just paid some guys to kidnap us.

At first the water was calm, with bugs hovering over the surface, and no one talked, except for the occasional barks from the leader at the stern and the constant sirenlike noise of the jungle. In some places the river was almost fifty yards across, other times it narrowed into a sliver, with gigantic trees casting everything into deep evening shadow. Vines dangled from high branches like elaborate chandeliers. We slipped through steep canyons of schist rock and limestone—the "grotesque pillars" that Morde had seen. Crocodiles lounged on sandbars. The jungle grew denser, like the jungle that I had read about in Morde's journals. I grew excited. White skeins of mist clung to everything like fake Christmas tree snow.

Something howled.

"What was that?"

"Monkeys," said Chris.

"It sounded like a huge wolf."

"They just sound big."

"Like the monkey men," I said. "The Ulaks." I looked up into the green canopy above, but there was nothing.

"Watch the river," Chris urged. He began, "You gotta—" but then stopped and pointed. Beginning as a distant clamor, the water soon began to roar, shutting out the din of the monkeys. Pancho emitted a cowboy yell. "Hold on!" We were about to hit rapids. I threw my notes into a Ziploc bag, and the bowman grabbed for his six-foot oar. Suddenly I felt the boat being sucked downstream, as if caught in a chute. The boat accelerated toward a minefield of rocks, the water churning a hard white. I grasped the wood gunwales just as the engine struck ground and then began to squeal as the stern jumped out of the water.

The river bent right and then left, and then, once through the minefield, we were heading for a jutting cliff face at a hundred miles per hour. It felt as though we were locked onto a rail, the way the boat was going straight for it. But what scared me most was that the bowman didn't move right away. He just stood there, a cigarette dangling from his mouth, a man prepared to die. "Rock!" I yelled, thinking that would get someone doing something. For a second I considered leaping overboard, even though I wasn't wearing a life jacket. But the bowman stabbed his oar into the white water and, in one hulking pull, sent the boat off in the other direction.

▾ ▾ ▾

AFTER TWO HOURS, we left the Río Cuyamel and entered the much wider Patuca, one of Central America's longest rivers. Once the Patuca leaves the highlands of Olancho, it skirts the Nicaraguan border and travels into the sticky swamps and unmarked jungles of the Mosquitia, where the Indians lived and the lost city was thought by many to be hidden. The river travels in a winding way for about 150 miles, then opens up, expanding in places to almost a mile wide, before dumping into the Caribbean Sea. One thing I had been told about the Patuca before I came was that it served as a superhighway for drug running and that small, bloody wars between the military and traffickers sometimes erupted along its waters. I heard about pitpans filled with cocaine and about an American fugitive who lived somewhere along the riverbanks. The Patuca was flooded. The river in similar shape had forced Morde to abandon his lost city. A gazillion side channels had opened up and were running out of the interior, ripping up entire trees and brush and sending them to threaten us as we motored downstream.

The rain hit, and for a good half hour we hunkered down under a black tarp. When I looked out again, the boat had been pulled ashore. "What are we doing?" I asked.

Chris groaned. "Got me." There was nothing around us but a crawling jungle.

The leader stepped out of the boat and shook the water off his sombrero. "Gringos," he said. He announced that he wasn't happy with the fee we had negotiated. His two sidekicks stood on either side of him now, unsmiling, hands on their waists. I felt that the situation was about to turn ugly. The leader spat. He wanted $300.

Chris tried reason, but the man shook his head and gestured at the high mountains. We paid him $200 in the end, but I still wasn't convinced that we were done. What was keeping him from demanding more—or just robbing us or even killing us and taking everything we owned? Surely our equipment, not to mention the thousand dollars we had stowed secretly in a plastic bag at the bottom of one bag, would be worth the risk of getting rid of us.

We went on but didn't get very far before the leader said, "We're not going any farther today." With night coming, he said, it was too dangerous to go on. "I'll take you the rest of the way tomorrow." We tried to argue, but there was no point. He nodded toward the top of a hill, which was covered in trees and creeping plant life, and steered the boat to shore. Protruding from the green hell was a wood hut with a metal roof. "We'll stay here tonight," he said.

▼ ▼ ▼

THE LEADER INTRODUCED himself as Ernesto. He was vague about what he did on the river. "It's interesting here," he said. "We do many things." He laughed and made a chopping gesture, as if he were throwing an ax at a tree trunk—or somebody's neck. Darkness had come, and we sat around a fire inside Ernesto's two-room hut and stared out at the cornfield he'd just planted and the impenetrable leafage beyond. The hut was made of fresh-cut pine, with raised wood floors. It was a palace compared with the other places we had slept in. At least five other men were in the shadows. Machetes and guns rested against one wall, and clothes hung from the rafters. This was Ernesto's little fiefdom.

Pancho and Angel excused themselves to set up our hammocks

outside as a young woman with black hair boiled coffee over the fire. "It gets very dark," said Ernesto, pointing at the clammy air around us. His gold teeth twinkled in the firelight. The woman handed us coffee, and for the most part we drank in silence before she and Ernesto withdrew to the second room. The moaning that followed could have been the two of them or the jungle.

"What do you think?" I asked Chris.

"It's gonna be a long night."

We were days from any paved road, and I was too tired to think about escaping. Where exactly would we walk? I couldn't have walked if I'd wanted to. For a moment I swore at myself for being so stupid. I had been on the road for almost two weeks now—through dusty cities, on buses and in 4×4s, through rivers, and over mountains. My pants were ripped, my boots shot. My blisters were now oozing a grayish milky liquid.

"I feel drugged."

"It's like that," Chris said. He had been hearing me complain for the last few days.

"I'm so fucking tired. I can't do this."

Chris shook his head.

"Hell," I said.

"Worse."

I was sick of beans and tortillas, sick of Clif Bars, sick of sweet fucking coffee. We dreamed out loud. "Cheeseburger," I said. Chris wanted Pizza Hut pizza with the works.

"Maybe I'd take a shower over food right now," I said, rethinking it, looking at my blackened hands. "A luxury hotel," I said.

I had tried to bathe in the river an hour before, imagining that the fresh rain-forest water would cleanse me—both wash away the physical dirt clinging to every inch of my body and clear away my mucked-up mind. But it hadn't gone as planned. I had stripped to my boxers and dunked my head under the muddy water but raised it when I felt a stick bump into my calf and shore up there. It was not a stick, however. It was brown like one but softer and rounder, with flecks of corn. One of Ernesto's men had gone upriver for his own private purge.

"Hell," I said again.

That's when Chris brought up the space suit. He did that when we'd been walking for miles through rain or when the sun was blasting or just when he felt us cracking.

"It would be air-conditioned," Chris said about the suit. "And sealed up, maybe motors to help you walk up the hills."

"Mine would have a jet pack," I said.

"And there would be a refrigerated panel for water," Chris said.

"And a satellite phone that actually worked."

"An LCD panel on the face of your helmet playing the best movies."

I asked Chris, "Why do you even do this?"

He laughed.

"I know," I said, "I've been doing stuff like this for years, dangerous things. But this is worse—the snakes, the airborne disease. Stuff you can't even control. This is awful."

"The people trying to kill you," he interjected as he looked at the shadows behind us. "It can be really tough here." He paused. "It's difficult to explain why I do it. It's not risk for its own sake."

"But this is risk," I said, gesturing at the shadows.

He said his sense of risk was probably a lot different from others'. When he went on trips, he usually had a reasonable expectation of making it back.

"Usually?"

"Of course, what's reasonable may be different to me than some others."

There had been one time, though, that had nearly gotten Chris to rethink that way of living. One summer he had come down with malaria, and as he lay in bed he thought he wasn't going to make it. Around that time he heard the news of a colleague who had been stung by a stingray and died. "It really hit home that what we do can exact a price," he said. But none of it ended up changing him. "The payoff is doing this—out here," he said.

I nodded. I wanted to believe it, that there was truly a purpose, that at least I would find the city that Morde found and be able to tell my family about it. That Amy would understand and that Sky would get why I wasn't a fireman at the station around the corner. But I couldn't think of any of that right now. "How bad do you think these guys are?" I wondered.

Chris shrugged. "I have no idea. But they don't look like good guys."

As he said that, two men appeared. The bigger one was Frog, the bowman. The other I had never seen. He was shorter and less muscular, with a white shirt open at the chest and faded jeans held up by a brass buckle the size of his fist. Had they been listening to us all this time? The toothless bowman laughed. "Gringos," he said.

"THE JUNGLE DOES NOT SEEM
LIKE IT WANTS US TO GO"

STANDING IN FRONT of a mirror, Morde didn't fully recognize the man staring back. His thick beard could be taken for tree bark. Two tropic ulcers had suddenly opened on his left leg, one the size of a half-dollar. What had the jungle done to him?

On the way down the Patuca, the men had decided to stop their canoe at the Germans' and clean up. It took Morde half an hour with the razor to see his old self—the man who had first come to this faraway place.

The next day, they reached the hut of the American exile George Brayton and pressed him for news about the war. Paris had fallen, and Hitler now controlled France. Brayton told them that the United States was sending aid money to Britain and that President Roosevelt was rumored to be contemplating joining the battle. The Americans were practically in the war.

The news lent Morde and Brown a sense of urgency. "We decided to . . . get back to La Ceiba before the war marooned us down here," Morde wrote.

A rainstorm held them up at Brayton's for a day, however, and they were further waylaid when a local boy arrived with urgent news. His mother had just died that morning, and a fever was quickly infecting his tiny forest village. He pleaded for the men's help. Without a second thought, Brown and Burke refused to venture into the "fever district" for any amount of money. They said it was crazy, the equivalent of a death sentence. Morde disagreed. "Since we had medicine that might possibly help," he wrote, "it was clearly a duty to render whatever assistance possible."

Morde grabbed his medical kit and slogged alongside the boy for four and a half miles through the muck. Secretly, he knew his mission was foolhardy, but he steeled himself with the knowledge that he was immunized against typhoid. The hot mud sucked at his rotting boots. Immediately he was more worried about the deadly creatures hidden among the shadows. "The fear of lurking snakes in such swamp served to take my mind off the fever danger for the time being," he wrote. Just outside the village, that changed. Human misery assailed his ears. The delirious cries and screams of the sickened could be heard plainly.

As he entered the village, the first thing he saw was a dead pig wedged into the drinking well, bobbing just underneath the slimy surface. The stench was overwhelming. It was the settlement's only water supply, and as far as Morde could tell the well was still in use. Trudging into the village, he covered his nose with a wet handkerchief.

In the village's ten thatched huts, Morde found twelve sick people. The boy introduced him as "the doctor." One man's urine was pink. Morde discovered a girl prone on the floor, "staring wildly." Some villagers had taken flight. Among those who stayed it was believed that an evil spirit had descended to wage a war.

The most obvious source of the sickness, Morde guessed, was the pig in the well. He believed that the tribespeople had contracted blackwater fever and instructed the village elder, who had just buried one of his daughters, to dig a new water supply and burn every sleeping mat and blanket.

Although Morde never specifically addressed in his notes why the tribespeople hadn't extracted the pig, he suggested that it had something to do with their fear of the evil spirit's presence in the corpse. Moving the pig, they thought, might further agitate the spirit. "In such cases," Morde reported, "the tribe often moves out entirely."

In the meantime, he gave the elder the antimalarial drug atabrine, which was also used to treat giardiasis, a disease caused by a tapewormlike intestinal parasite. At first the elder was a bit suspicious of the pills. He held one pill in his palm, eyeing it as if he had never seen such a thing before, as if Morde was asking him to swallow a stone. To show them it wasn't poison, Morde took a dose himself, and that was enough to change the man's mind. "So torn was he by grief and fear, the elder accepted my advice and medicine without hesitation," Morde wrote.

He spent the day working with the sick people. "I made the rounds, feeling foreheads and pulses and watching to make sure the pills were taken. Several victims resisted and were made to swallow forcibly."

When he turned to go, he was hopeful that he had done some good, that he had maybe even saved a life.

▾ ▾ ▾

AFTER MORDE REUNITED with Brown and Burke, they continued on as fast as they could for a week and a half. The mountains melted away into swamp, then savannas and cattle fields, then swamp again. Bugs attacked with such intensity and profusion that they sounded like the "engine of an airplane." They encountered more rapids. Then one night, as they slept on a sandbar, they woke in a panic to see that the river had swept away their canoe, along with everything in it—their equipment, the journals, the map to the lost city. Four months of exploring gone. All night they searched the "black emptiness" that was the river. With no energy to go on, Morde battled thoughts of dying. He couldn't walk anymore. He didn't sleep. "The jungle does not seem like it wants us to go," Morde wrote. It wasn't until the next morning that he and Burke located the boat. Miraculously, it had been snagged on a bank a mile downstream. Although it was upright and everything was intact, Morde was still spooked. "It was a moment of utter despair," he wrote. "One of the lowest of the trip."

Twenty-five hours later, on June 26, they heard the softly thudding waves of the sea.

"PLEASE COME HOME"

THE TRIP HAD long ago taken on the senseless logic of broken sleep, with no clear division between night and day. It felt a lot like those first months when Sky was a newborn, my brain so sleep deprived, it was hard to ever tell if I was awake or dreaming. We didn't pay attention anymore to the time, only the sun as it came and went in the jungle. We were getting closer to the White City, or whatever Morde had found, but there were still days to go.

Pancho's burbling radio provided a constant parallel narrative of the coup. The morning we woke up at Ernesto's, there was more news of the exiled president forming a private army at the Nicaraguan border, about ten hours' walk from us. Diplomatic talks had broken down. Meanwhile, the male announcer reported that the United States continued to reject the coup's legitimacy and was calling for all humanitarian aid to be cut off.

Later, as we waited for the pirates to wake up, the news program morphed into a kind of personal message board, where the announcer read letters in a slow musical voice that exuded the feeling of a long sung poem. Pancho put his finger to his lips. It was the most popular show in the jungle region. For people who lived off the grid, without telephones, there was no more effective way to communicate with the world around you and beyond. Some messages were love letters; others were requests or notices.

A mother named Maria missed her son, who had moved to La Ceiba for work; a man named José announced the birth of a daughter; another man pleaded for a doctor; Reyes, a young man, said he was delayed in Tegucigalpa and would arrive home early the following week with a phone charger; another needed a boat to take his goods down the Río Negro; and a woman grieved the death of her mother the day before and urged her siblings to "Please come home."

All of it reminded me that I needed to call Sky. It was her birthday. From Chris's bag, I grabbed the satellite phone and flipped it on. It searched and searched for a signal, but it wouldn't connect, even when I walked to the top of a hill and then down to the river edge. I didn't even know what time it was. Were they still asleep? That reminded me of the raccoon. I imagined Amy the night before lying in Sky's narrow bedroom, which was right next to ours, her eyes open, listening for any stray movements in the pitch dark. The thoughts of them at home and the way I waited and waited for the satellite phone to get through made the great distance between us seem maddeningly unbridgeable.

"ICE IN OUR GLASSES!"

BREWER'S LAGOON WAS a rough-and-tumble pioneer town on the Mosquito Coast with a spattering of shabby wattle-and-daub huts topped with tin or leaves. An American named Frank Jones put the three men up for the night. In Morde's description, Jones was "long, lean and nervous with pale eyes which smile so easily you wouldn't take him for a killer."

A friend of Burke, Jones was a hired gun for local companies. "I lived for years [in Honduras] only by the grace of a quick trigger finger," he admitted as the men talked past midnight. "I've killed six men, but they had to be killed."

The confession made Morde and Brown uneasy. They had escaped the jungle, and now they were crashing with a killer. But the two explorers were too weary to act on those concerns. "We were so tired," Morde wrote, "that we would have slept in a den of snakes."

▼ ▼ ▼

SEVERAL DAYS LATER, on July 4, Morde and Brown left the Coast of Lost Hope—a melancholic name that Burke had bestowed on the out-of-the-way place. They gave much of their equipment to Burke, as they'd promised. With them on board the La Ceiba–bound boat was their bird, Pete. As the ship sailed out to sea, Brown and Morde watched the land fade away until darkness eclipsed the whole scene.

"We slept on a hatch under the stars all night," he wrote in his last entry from that territory. Any sadness Morde felt looking back at the hundreds of miles they had traveled centered on Burke. "One regret is that Burke never even said thank you or goodbye," Morde wrote. They would never see him again.

At 4 a.m., the men woke to their first glimpse of civilization—the lights of La Ceiba. The two friends returned to the Paris Hotel, where for the first time in more than three months they enjoyed the simple luxury of a bed and the clean smell of its soft, freshly laundered cotton sheets. There were other comforts too: "First got a coca cola, a barber shop shave . . . ice in our glasses!"

The days before their return to the United States were a blur of activity. Morde met with the U.S. consul and then traveled to Tegucigalpa, the dusty Honduran capital, where he visited with President Tiburcio Carías Andino and the cartographer Dr. Jesús Aguilar Paz. Fourteen years later, Aguilar Paz would produce the first official map of the country with its famous question mark, along with the notation "Ruinas Ciudad Blanca" stamped on a stretch of mostly unexplored territory in the eastern part of the country—above the Río Wampú.

Finally, on July 20, the men located a fruit ship, the *Patria*, heading to Tampa, Florida. They paid the captain $40 for two spots among the roughneck sailors and bade Honduras good-bye. After six nights at sea and four months of travel, Theodore Morde's Honduran expedition was at last going home.

ERNESTO'S STORY

HEY GUARD IT with their life. They war with others. They
are not like they were. They war with themselves. They kill each
other. It is a *secreto*. You know that?"

We were gliding along the river now, and Ernesto was telling us
about the Tawahkas, the tribe that inhabited the banks of the Patuca.

Most of the Tawahkas are Catholic, as the tribe long ago fell under
the spell of missionaries. Observers have lately described the tribe as
"endangered," like the nearby Pech, though the population was up
from its low of 160 at the turn of the century. Tawahkas were leaving
or marrying into other tribes and sometimes fighting one another.

Bloods mixed; traditions dimmed and were forgotten. In 1940,
Morde had reported that there were fifteen full-blooded Tawahkas in
one camp. Today, there are fewer than ten full-blooded Tawahkas in
five villages. The government had passed laws protecting the tribes
from the outside world pushing in, converting their land into a "biosphere reserve." But the police and military were a long way away;
hence the tribe's need to be protective of their lives, what they own,
the histories and traditions and legends they cling to.

The rain clouds had now dispersed, leaving behind twists of fog
floating over the dimness. Howler monkeys groaned, their combined
noises like a distant hurricane working up to force. Frog, in his muscle

shirt, plied the engine. There were three of them, all packing their guns, and a young boy whom I had not seen the night before.

Ernesto had joined Chris and me in the bow. He knew what we were searching for. Ernesto's man had told him about our conversation the night before.

"You must be careful about what Indians you talk to about that," he said. "It's a *secreto.*" Extracting a plastic lighter from his pocket, he lit a hand-rolled cigarette and then flapped his cigarette hand at the dense wall of woods around us as if he were waving off a mosquito cloud.

"I have a friend who heard some things from the Indians and went out there looking," he said. He nudged close to us, his gold teeth glinting in the sun, which had just emerged from the mess of morning fog. "He had been walking for two days," he said. "He started finding beautiful pottery. Grinding stones, pieces of things. There were drawings on rocks—monkeys and people and circles. These were signs."

Ernesto paused while we took this in. On the left riverbank, I noticed a lonely hut on stilts, the first sign of habitation in many hours. Pancho and Angel stared off into the distance, listening to their radio, as Ernesto's men watched us.

Just as Ernesto was about to go on, a tree limb slammed into the side of the boat. "You see that?" he asked.

"The tree?"

"No," he said. "The jungle. It wasn't just a tree." He flicked away his dying cigarette and smiled at us as if we were suddenly in this trip together, a shift in mood from last night.

"The painted rocks," he said, picking up his story. "He followed them for three more days. He said he felt close to the ruins."

"What part of the jungle?" I asked.

"Out there," he said. "It doesn't matter where." He put his hands around his neck and stuck out his tongue, which was blobby and black like the gunk from the bottom of the river.

"Whatever he heard from the Indians was wrong," he said. "He grew sick. He could hardly walk." He spat into the water before finishing. "The sickness was all over him. His head, stomach, feet. He had to turn back."

Only then did the man start to feel better. After a day of walking away, Ernesto said, the sickness vanished and from that day forward he would never again venture into the jungle.

▼ ▼ ▼

WHEN I'D SET out, I had imagined writing a book that might show my daughter what kind of man I was, how I had grappled with the big questions of life—getting older, leaving youth behind, commitments, the importance of experience and discovery, and even love. Instead I was fumbling through the jungle, falling apart, nearly dying. It was the opposite of strong.

I grieved, in a way. I had gone from feeling lost at home to being literally lost in this jungleland. I wasn't even sure there was anything to discover. What if Morde had been lying? What if the city didn't exist? More and more the question crept into my mind. Even if it did exist, this jungle was a rabbit hole that opened up into scores of other rabbit holes. You could walk for months and months, slashing and hacking and climbing, and not see the same damn place twice. Except it all looked the same to me.

For a stretch I tried to jot down my thoughts, describe the sound of the river passing by, and it calmed my mind a bit. I wrote about Sky asking me about socks in the jungle and tried to hang on.

▼ ▼ ▼

WITH NO BOTTLED water, we relied on the river and iodine drops, which made everything taste like iron. We passed the first Tawahka camp, where Morde had likely stopped, back when the camp boasted about twenty-four huts and a school. Now there was only tall grass. In October 1998, Hurricane Mitch had struck the site and swept everything away. Farther downstream, Ernesto directed the boat into a Tawahka settlement known as Yapuwas. His men decided to follow us up the steep dirt path to the village. I had heard them whispering to one another as we got off the boat, which made me think that they were coming along for information we might turn up.

"This isn't good," I said to Chris.

"Let's just see how it plays out. Watch."

One carried a rifle, which he held with both hands, allowing for a quick shot. There was no one around, but it felt as if there were a hundred eyes staring out from the dozen or so huts. The huts straddled a dirt track. They were in various stages of decay, with rotting boards and thatched roofs that looked animal gnawed. Some appeared abandoned. The only sound was the loud buzzing of cicadas.

Ernesto called out with something like a birdcall, and after a considerable hiatus four women in old skirts emerged from behind one of the huts. Two young boys in cut-off jeans followed. Ernesto's man steadied his gun. We said hello, and the women nodded, though their faces remained expressionless. When we asked if there was anyone here who could talk to us, they shook their heads. One woman said that the men were out in the fields and wouldn't be back until nightfall.

When we mentioned Ciudad Blanca, there was a protracted silence. Then a young boy, wearing no shoes, stepped forward. "I know about it," he said in Spanish, but the women stopped him, whispering something in their native tongue, and that was the end of our encounter.

We walked once through the small village, with the women watching us, before we decided to keep going. Ernesto and his men did the same. Any imaginings they'd had of secret information leading to stores of gold or buried artifacts ended. Before he left, Ernesto said, "Good luck," with a chuckle. He hadn't noticed Pancho speaking to the Indian boy, who'd said a man at the next Tawahka camp could help us. "He knows many things," the boy said. He told us to ask simply for "the elder."

"THIS STRANGE CIVILIZATION"

ON THE MORNING of August 2, 1940, Theodore Morde arrived at the Biltmore Hotel to tell his incredible story. The hotel was one of Manhattan's stateliest, with two brick towers and a subterranean concourse opening to a platform for the luxury Chicago express 20th Century Limited train—"the world's greatest," according to the *New York Times*. A crowd of reporters turned out, eager to hear all about the lost city. Reporters were present from the *New York Times*, the *New York Herald Tribune*, the *New York Sun*, and the Associated Press. Morde, twenty-eight pounds lighter, had come by train from Tampa. In photographs, he wears a double-breasted khaki suit, his hair swept back and shiny with pomade and a slender mustache that makes him look a bit like Clark Gable. Standing in front of the flashing cameras that morning, he projected the air of a man who had just returned from another planet. The jungle had imbued him with a palpable mystery.

One reporter would describe Morde's discovery as "romantic," a welcome departure from the grim mood gripping the city. Having spread across Europe, World War II had seized the collective psyche of New York and the country at large. The *New York Times* was reporting the "scythe-like sweep" of Hitler's German army. There was concern that once the führer finished with Britain he would sail his soldiers across the Atlantic to besiege the United States. National conscription was under consideration, and a city commission of engineers had been charged with fashioning defensive measures for possible gas attacks and bombings. Meanwhile, Mayor Fiorello La Guardia worked to fortify the spirits of a population suffering 15 percent unemployment.

"A big part of our job was charting rivers and streams which no white man had ever traversed before," Morde told the crowd. "We spent weeks poling tediously up tangled jungle streams." He paused, taking in all the eyes on him. "When we could go no further, we started hacking a path through the jungle. It was tough going. There was a type of tiger claw bamboo that was full of thorns, and we could hardly get near enough to cut the branches away." He relished the attention as he recounted the wild's daunting obstacles: "dangers of isolation, disease, rains, devastating floods, and venomous snakes." He told of the wild pigs that had nearly killed him as well as the deadly fer-de-lance. He said, "We had to eat wild boar, deer, and dragon-like iguana lizards. Our only vegetable was wild banana—generally cooked green." At one point, he reached into his suit pants and produced a gleaming vial of gold. It was a land of incredible riches, he said. He called Honduras an "oil-bearing land" with deposits of silver and platinum. About the gold, he said, "We picked this up with our own bare hands."

The reporters wanted to know about the city, but Morde was cagey in his answers. He said that his expedition had returned with traces of an ancient kingdom dating back to "before Christ was born," including several hundred artifacts, from pottery to a pitpan, which would be displayed at George Heye's National Museum of the American Indian. He pronounced the capital city's name for the scrum: the Lost City of the Monkey God. He had said the name many times to himself by now. It was a civilization, he said, "whose people had learned to build with stone and who worshipped monkeys as gods."

Stepping toward the clamoring reporters, he told them that the city was a buried, distant place with a long, ancient wall disappearing into the centuries-old murk. Crude roads lined with stone buildings had once radiated outward through the verdure. "All that was left," he went on, "were mounds of earth covering crumbling walls where houses once stood as stone foundations of what may have been majestic temples."

He elaborated on his theory that the monkey capital had perhaps at one time been home to thousands of people—maybe up to thirty thousand—and that the inhabitants had likely been contemporaries of the Maya. "I saw a great jungle-covered mound which, when some day we excavate it, I believe may reveal a monkey deity," he said. "I found a facial mask. . . . It looked like the face of a monkey. . . . On nearly everything we found was carved the likeness of the monkey—the monkey god. What it stood for, I don't know, but some day they will be deciphered and we will know the whole story of this strange civilization."

Morde wouldn't go into details about the city's location. He was afraid that people would plunder the site in his absence and disrupt a future excavation. As for the existence of the smelted gold goblets and dishes, like the Indian princess had mentioned to the Spanish bishop Pedraza in 1545, Morde didn't talk about that either.

▼ ▼ ▼

THE *NEW YORK TIMES* published two stories, highlighting "evidence of a thriving agricultural civilization" that had been "wiped out by some major catastrophe." The other prominent daily, the *New York Sun*, reported how "the people of that almost inaccessible spot were highly developed and very likely representative of an advanced civilization," an assertion that helped Morde's case against the long-entrenched narrative that a major farming civilization could never flourish in a rain forest.

Morde was twenty-nine years old and that day walked away from the Biltmore a kind of legend: a man who had gone to a place where few men had dared to go before. Just as people around the world were feeling edgy and threatened, Morde gave them reason to dream again, to imagine going to a distant place and glimpsing the traces of another age. An op-ed in the *Standard Tribune* put it this way: "The world of ours has been pretty well explored since the days when map makers could show only the Mediterranean littoral and filled in the rest of their maps with pictures of sea monsters. Yet the fact that there are still things waiting to be discovered is brought home to us in Theodore Morde. . . . A discovery like his will add to mankind's knowledge of the world's past."

Meanwhile, Manhattan high society feted him. What was it like there? they asked. Did the natives try to kill you? A monkey cult? How much gold did you find? Women gravitated to him, intrigued by his bravery, pulled in by his handsome movie-star looks. But none of them could pin him down. He reunited with his sponsor, George Heye, and presented him with hundreds of artifacts. There is no record of their conversation, but it likely entailed Heye's favorite subject, "the great mystery of the origin of the prehistoric races of the Western Hemisphere."

The mystery of the city was the subject of Morde's lecture at the legendary Explorers Club, where other adventurers including Percy Fawcett and Charles Lindbergh had told their tales. He appeared on radio shows, on college campuses, and at the World's Fair in Flushing, Queens, where he was photographed at the telephone exhibit with a pretty, dark-haired woman. Later, he published his *American Weekly* story. The Hearst publication boasted, ridiculously, 50 million readers. Titled "In the Lost City of Ancient America's Monkey God," the cover line was breathless: "Explorer Theodore Morde Finds in Honduras Jungles a Vanished Civilization's Prehistoric Metropolis, Where Sacrifices Were Made to the Gigantic Idol of an Ape—and Describes the Weird 'Dance of the Dead Monkeys' Still Practiced by Natives in Whom Runs the Olden Blood."

In his syndicated column, "New York Day by Day," Charles B. Driscoll observed Morde's "uncommonly handsome person." "In white Palm Beach suit, immaculate white shirt and white shoes," Driscoll continued, "he seemed to me the last person in the diningroom I'd have picked as the man who discovered the romantic City of the Monkey God, in Central American wilds." In the same interview, Morde's fellow explorer and mentor Captain Stuart Murray said he was impressed by his protégé's superhuman abilities: "I hunted for that city for years. This fellow found it on his first try."

▼ ▼ ▼

MORDE RETURNED HOME to New Bedford to see his family in the fall of 1940. It had been many years since he had first stood at the end of his block, near the harbor, and stared out at the ocean, wondering what the world held for him. He gave his sister two cups of gold that he had prospected from the rivers. The memory of Morde's old life, who he was before he'd left on that cruise ship as a stowaway in his teens, before he'd left for the Spanish war, and then the jungle, all of that receded. It was hard for his family to keep up with him. In his absence, he had become a different person. He was now a grown man. He told his family stories about his travels. But it was impossible for him to explain everything. Many things were simply untranslatable. He said he was thinking of writing a book, but right now he didn't have any time.

The *New Bedford Standard*, which had been following Morde's traveling life over the years, interviewed him at length. After all the news stories recounting his adventures, Morde felt that he needed to clear something up. "Being interested in archaeology, as I naturally have been because of my travels to most of the famous ruins of the world, does not make me an archaeologist any more than my three months in Spain made me, as some interviewers described me, a war correspondent," he said. "I think being termed an explorer would suffice."

When the reporter inquired about his plans to return to the city, Morde replied that with the help of George Heye he had already been at work organizing an expedition for January 1941. In his travel notes, he had mapped out a flat place in the forest, in the eastern part of the country, where a landing strip could be chopped out. Planes would be able to fly in supplies and a larger team. A dam could be set up to provide drinking water. As for timing, he expected it to take years to uncover the site.

Later, on a radio show, he encouraged the mystery of his return and said he had so many questions. "What happened to the people who lived there?" he asked. "Why did they, a highly civilized race, vanish from the face of the earth? No one knows. But I hope soon to find out. I'm going back to the City of the Monkey God, to try to solve one of the few remaining mysteries of the Western World."

None of that happened, however. By winter, still a year before the United States was actually attacked, talk of war escalated. There was military draft legislation and rumors of rations. President Roosevelt supported Great Britain with arms, suggesting a tilt toward intervention, and, as men began preparing for service, the birthrate climbed. Then an urgent call came to Morde from Washington: a new clandestine government office needed his services for a special mission that would be just as mysterious as his trip to the lost city. Morde was about to disappear again, this time to become a spook.

WHAT WE LEARNED
FROM THE TAWAHKAS

THE FIRST CERTAIN clue that we were finally onto Morde's lost-city trail was the sight of Howler Monkey Mountain. The Tawahkas called it Quicungun. It stood at the confluence of the Patuca and Wampú rivers in the shape of a ruined temple—gigantic, engorged in trees, shrouded in mist. Howler monkeys growled from the shade. At no other point had I heard them so clearly, even though I could not see them. You could hear them for miles, disembodied, their guttural screams echoing off the water and the cliffs.

It was drizzling as we stood at the Tawahka village of Krautara, which Morde had likely passed through nearly seventy years before. In his notes, the explorer had written that the mountain appeared to be "rearing its bulk." A floppy-haired Tawahka teenager named José told us that the mountain had once caught fire. "It burned orange and red for a week. Then it died out," he said. "The elders said it was the spirits talking. But I don't know." He shrugged.

One thing I have noticed only in retrospect, mostly from reading other books about the jungle, was that we rarely, if ever, spoke about the beauty of the forest, like the misty green mountain in front of us. I was always too tired or too scared or too discombobulated to consider anything beyond my physical suffering and the purpose at hand.

The elder we had come to see about the lost city was off hunting, so José invited us to his hut on the hill to meet someone else while we waited. Krautara was one of the larger Tawahka settlements dotting the Patuca. There were two other towns on the lower stretches of the river—Wampusirpi and Krausirpi—and the only way to reach them was by boat; no roads or airstrips connected them to the outside world. In Krautara, about ten wood huts with thatched or metal roofs straddled a muddy path. Although it had been bigger by five or ten huts when Morde came, the village now had a concrete schoolhouse and a soccer field.

José's house was one room with a porch that overlooked the river. We sat on wood benches opposite one another. José wore a yellow cotton vest opened at his bony chest and faded jeans, held up around his slender waist by a brass buckle the size of a playing card. He swept his wet black hair out of his face and in broken Spanish that Chris translated he asked where we were from.

"New York," I said.

"Is that near Italy?"

"It's in America," I said.

"Can you walk to Italy from there?"

I explained that Italy was across the Atlantic Ocean in Europe. At that his face brightened. "Rambo!" he said and pulled at a cross hanging from his neck. "Rambo is in America? I love that movie." He made the universal sign for a machine gun. "I watched that many times until our TV broke," he said. That had been two or three years before.

Meanwhile, Pancho and Angel had wandered off to explore the surroundings. Angel seemed less anxious now that the pirates had departed. In the distance, I could hear him toying with his cell phone's ringtones. His father, however, was somber. His radio had died, and he had no news of the coup to occupy him. Upon our arrival, he said he wasn't convinced that the pirates had really left us behind and feared an ambush. He also seemed to be dwelling on his imminent return to his old village. Over the past few days I'd noticed him breaking off from us and walking away to stare at the river or a hole in the greenery, picking up a flower or gazing up at the bulk of a towering mahogany tree. Like he was reacquainting himself with the wilderness that had once expelled him and seeking its permission to return.

As the rain came down harder, pinging the metal roof, another man stopped in. He introduced himself as "the teacher" and said his name was Dixon. He was "around thirty-seven," shirtless, with muscle-ripped arms and a buzz cut that made his head look like a hammer. Like José, he had been born in Krautara and had not traveled very far from the river. "I've never been to New York!" he said. But he wondered what it was like "out there."

The Tawahka people continued to exist mainly as hunter-gatherers and traded a few crops and gold along the river. When I asked Dixon about his tribe's history, he pointed at his shaved head, where the story of the Tawahkas resided. I remembered that the Tawahka chief had said the same thing to Morde. There were still no books, no archives. Chris smiled. "Like Homer," he said.

Dixon said his ancestry stretched back thousands of years, but his tribe felt threatened. He mentioned the Spanish conquistadors—the beheadings, the enslavement, the murders of Indians. About that, there was a legend that had been passed down over the centuries. "There was a great earthquake after the Spanish came," he said. "It destroyed one of the bigger cities. And in part of that city there was a great temple of gold." He paused. "When the earthquake hit, there was a landslide. The mountain came down and covered the city. Now no one knows where it is."

I asked him how many of his tribe remained. "We were once a very large city along the river." he said. "We were almost five thousand. Now we are all spread out, and there are less than a thousand."

Lately, heavily armed settlers and ranchers were terrorizing them.

"Bad, bad," he said, pointing at the swirling clouds overhead, as if to suggest that violence had settled into their territory like a storm front. "They take everything."

▾　▾　▾

WE ATE A dinner of beans and tortillas with an unrecognizable white meat in a hut belonging to a woman who lived at the center of the village. In a corner, a fire warmed the cool night air. Not long afterward, the old man we were looking for returned, the wooden grip of a knife sticking out of his belt. He nodded at us. He was soaked from the storm. His white button-down stuck to his chest. His jeans were falling off his waist, and his tall rubber boots were thick with miles of mud. His face was embedded with wrinkles, and a tuft of white hair sprouted off his chin. His name was Marcos, but people referred to him as the chief, or cacique.

We walked over to his hut, which was elevated on stilts. The interior was unadorned. There was a bed made of tree branches, some clothes folded neatly on the floor, and a framed black-and-white picture of his deceased mother and father that a photographer had taken many years before.

After he changed into dry clothes, Marcos sat on a wood chair and showed me the blackened tooth around his neck. "It is from a jaguar I killed a long time ago," he said in Spanish. He laughed, as if the thought of his younger days amused him. He said he was one of the oldest living Indians there and thought he had been born in 1929. "But I don't know for certain." He smiled, no teeth, as a middle-aged woman arrived with a tray of steaming sweet coffee.

"It was a good time then," he reminisced about his boyhood as rain struck the metal roof. "There were many animals. Tapirs, jaguars, pigs." He stretched his arms as far as he could to show the size of the fish he'd caught, sometimes with his bare hands, other times with a spear. "You could go out and hunt or fish and always come back with something," he said, as if describing a grocery store. "But now it is much harder to find the animals." That day he'd caught nothing, but he was planning to go back out the next day.

I told him about Theodore Morde and asked if he had any memory of the expedition. Marcos would have been about eleven years old then. He thought for a moment but said he wasn't sure. "I've seen many gringos looking for things," he said with a smile. He remembered the Germans whom Morde had visited on the Patuca and their barge. "They're gone, and so is their banana plantation," he said. He remembered the American exile Brayton too. He'd vanished. "Gone," he said.

When I asked if there were any large ancient ruins in the area, Marcos stared at me, as if trying to determine my intention. He said there were old cities, but he stayed away from them. "People do not go there." Just then thunder struck and the old man lifted his eyes skyward. I mentioned Ciudad Blanca, and he took a sip of his coffee. "I will tell you what my parents told me," he said after some time. "Our ancestors used to live there. But bad people came, and they began killing each other. The bad people expelled our people. They had special powers—arrows that could be shot in the air and would hit whatever they wanted to hit. They could look at birds, and they would die."

Marcos set his cup down on the wood plank floor, which had been ground down over time to have the smooth surface of a bowling ball, and he sucked in the wet air. He said that the city was "beautiful." When I brought up Morde's description of a monkey dance, he shook his head. He remembered nothing like that. Later, however, another Tawahka man would say that there had once been a ritual of the sort, though he couldn't recall specific details, except that monkeys were eaten. The second Tawahka had also heard stories from his grandfather that there were three different types of fierce monkeys that inhabited the forest around Ciudad Blanca and protected what was inside its walls. "They don't allow anyone to get close to it," he said, wagging a withered finger. "And there is also a jaguar bigger than you've ever seen." He also warned us to stay away.

As the night wound down, I asked Marcos if he knew the location of the lost city. Slowly he unfolded himself from the chair and stood up. "There are many ancient things in the jungle," he reiterated. "But we don't touch them." I recalled the Indians who had abandoned Morde deep in the forest. Marcos inhaled deeply as he stared off toward Howler Monkey Mountain, now buried in darkness. I worried that I had offended him. He spoke the city's name. "It is up the Wampú," he finally said. "That is the place where my parents used to talk about." I repeated what he'd said. This was a crucial moment. "Up the Wampú," he said again, nodding toward the river. "It was the most sacred place."

▾ ▾ ▾

"A FAKE-OUT," I said to Chris later that night. We were lying in our hammocks, which were tied to railings outside the schoolhouse. The rain continued, and there was no moon. The darkness was of the sort you glimpse at the back of a cave. The satellite phone still didn't work. I'd missed Sky's fourth birthday without even speaking to her. Now she was probably in bed, asleep after all the sugar.

"That's what it looks like," he said.

In his notes, Morde had written that there was "no great civilization up the Wampu." But he had also noted that he was aware of ancient metate rolling stones (the rolling pin–like stones used to grind corn) discovered over a mountain range "far in from the Wampu and closer to the Plátano."

The two statements seemed odd together. There were artifacts scattered about the jungle above the Wampú, suggesting habitation and perhaps even an advanced people; it was up the Wampú where Captain Murray, Morde's predecessor, had heard tales of ruins.

But for some unknown reason Morde had declared that he wouldn't be going up the river to investigate. At least that is what he seemed to want any unwelcome readers of his journal to believe.

"Morde was lying," I said. "Just not in the way we thought."

Illustration by Laura Hartman Maestro ©2012

PART IV

White-lipped peccary

Río Plátano

Río Plátano Biosphere Reserve

Río Plátano

White City ?

"Ruinas Ciudad Blanca"

?

Río Paulaya

Bonanza

Howler monkey

Río Pao

Las Crucitas

Cielo Azul

Coral snake

Río Aner

Río Wampú

Río Wampú

Río Wampú

Begins foot trail

Río Patuca

From Krautara backtracks to Río Wampú in aluminum boat

Tawahka camp

— ◄- - - - ◄- - Stewart
● Locations approximate
〰〰〰 Country border
〜〜〜 River

Patuca

HONDURAS

Río Coco

NICARAGUA

Eladio's house

Río Cuyamel

Río Blanco

Camp Ulak

DAISY

IN **1943, THE** city of Istanbul was a zone of intrigue for both Allied and Axis actors—a hive of spies, double-crossers, hit men, and resistance groups. Turkey, at the nexus of two continents, was neutral in the war. The war took a turn that year. Hitler had just been driven out of Africa, Benito Mussolini's regime was in tatters, and the Soviets had retaken Stalingrad. Roosevelt promised the Allies an additional 10 million soldiers. In July, the Allies unleashed the largest aerial assault yet on the Third Reich, nearly leveling the city of Hamburg and killing 42,000 people. Winston Churchill declared that the goal was "to set Europe ablaze."

During that phase of the war, in the fall, Theodore Morde was making his way toward Istanbul "under the disguise," as he termed it in classified reports, "of a correspondent." For whom he didn't say, but sometimes he told people that he worked for *Reader's Digest*, which may or may not have been true. The magazine, with its numerous international bureaus, was rumored to provide cover for spies.

By now, Morde's jungle scruff was gone, and he had regained the weight he'd lost on the expedition. As a secret agent, he had to blend in wherever he went. He wore fitted suits and shiny shoes, sometimes with a thin, manicured mustache. There was another thing: in the field, he was no longer Theodore Morde. His code name was Daisy.

Thirty-two years old, Morde was three years out of the jungle and again loose in the world. He had spent the last few years bouncing from one undercover war assignment to another—Gibraltar, China, Syria, "the length and breadth of Africa." Although the war was meant to be only a hiatus from the search for the lost city, it became an extension of it too—a continuation of his adventuring self.

The year before he had been named to *Who's Who in America*, along with Bob Hope, and in New York, he was inducted into the Explorers Club, among other members like the Antarctic explorer Sir Ernest Henry Shackleton and Charles Lindbergh. Sporadically, he had lived in a houseboat on the Nile in Cairo.

But tracking him after he left Honduras in any kind of detailed way is difficult, if not out of the question. According to his classified personnel file, Morde was in "charge of many cases of espionage-sabotage." In his line of business, a paper trail was almost nonexistent, except for his field reports, which he sent by coded wire to Washington or to the local bureaus.

It was October when Morde finally landed in Istanbul. He had spent the last couple of months chasing shadowy links to Nazi Germany: through Algiers, Egypt, Syria, and now Turkey, where he believed that he had finally identified a contact with a supposedly firm tie to Adolf Hitler's inner circle. Morde's goal: to use this man to help with the assassination or capture of the führer. What was probably the most secretive assignment of his life began with an agent known only as Snapdragon.

▼ ▼ ▼

MORDE MET SNAPDRAGON at a nondescript office building perched on the shimmering Golden Horn. It was still early in the morning. He knew almost nothing about the agent. The man could be an enemy, and he wouldn't even know.

Standing in the mostly empty lobby of the building, he introduced himself as Daisy. Morde wore a dark gray pin-striped suit and a white button-down, projecting the image of an "all-American" from the "Ivy League," as the scene was recalled in Anthony Cave

Brown's book *Wild Bill Donovan* about the pre-CIA spy outfit known as the Office of Strategic Services (OSS).

At the outset, Snapdragon was shocked that Morde wanted to get in touch with one of Germany's most powerful men: Franz von Papen, the country's ambassador to Turkey. "It shouldn't surprise you," Snapdragon said, "that I'm not in the habit of arranging meetings for total strangers who wish to fraternize with the enemy."

Morde handed the agent a sheet of thin tissue with a typewritten list of details about a covert scheme involving the help of German turncoats to assassinate Hitler and force the Axis powers to surrender to the Allies. It was special paper—a splash of water or spit could disintegrate it, erasing all evidence of the encounter. Holding it in his hands, Snapdragon seemed confused. "Who in the hell," he asked, "sent you on this goddamn fool's errand?"

"It's no fool's errand," said Morde, holding his ground. "I was sent here by FDR." He then produced a letter from a high-level OSS agent, urging Snapdragon "to hold nothing back" from Morde, and eventually Snapdragon backed down. He agreed to put Morde in touch with the enemy but told him that he could not predict what would happen. He told Morde to be very careful, and then he was gone.

▼ ▼ ▼

FEW PEOPLE KNEW exactly when and how Morde joined the intelligence ranks. Officially, it was December 1940, before the OSS was born, but it could have been much earlier. Some suggested that George Heye, rumored to have connections to spy circles, had recruited him. Later, another of Heye's museum employees would join the black operatives. It is also possible that Morde had been working informally in some intelligence role as far back as the Spanish Civil War in the 1930s and even through his time searching for the lost city.

Whatever the truth, Morde was one of the first. The ranks of the OSS seemed to be a natural place for an adventurer like him. As a *Washington Times-Herald* columnist once put it, the agency had recruited "ex–polo players, millionaires, Russian princes, society gambol boys, scientists and dilettante detectives. . . . And the girls? The prettiest, best-born, snappiest girls." Some of the spies and spy staffers would later become famous, from Arthur Schlesinger Jr., to future Supreme Court justice Arthur Goldberg and the movie director John Ford, as well as Julia Child.

Formed after Pearl Harbor, in 1941, the agency was run by the quixotic ex–army colonel William Donovan. Donovan was known as "Wild Bill," a moniker he had earned during World War I when he had stood in the middle of a battlefield and, as all of his men crouched in fear behind a bunker, charged the enemy alone—and taken machine-gun fire to his leg.

Donovan called the OSS a "league of gentlemen"; later it would become the CIA. Early on, the agency was chaotic but also a bit idyllic for its operatives—"our springtime years," as one former OSS agent called them. Although Donovan considered the agency's main functions to be mining secrets from behind enemy lines and recruiting resistance forces, the colonel placed few limitations on his spies. "In a global and totalitarian war," he once said, "intelligence must be global and totalitarian." There were assassination attempts and kooky plots to promote uprisings (airdropping pictures of succulent food into starved German villages, for instance), as well as even more far-fetched attempts to alter the brains and bodies of foreign leaders (injecting Hitler's food with female hormones, for example).

Winston Churchill, whose Secret Intelligence Service was thought to be a model for Donovan's OSS, once described those fledgling spy days for the United States and Europe as "the most fantastic inventions of romance and melodrama. Tangle within tangle, plot and counter-plot, ruse and treachery, cross and double-cross, true agent, false agent, double agent, gold and steel, the bomb, the dagger and the firing party, were interwoven in many a texture so intricate as to be incredible and yet true."

Between 1928 and 1937, Theodore Morde circled the globe five times. *(Courtesy of Dave Morde)*

Did the White City exist? I was about to find out. *(Courtesy of the author)*

Amy said it felt as if I were going to the moon; Sky told me to watch out for crocodiles. *(Courtesy of the author)*

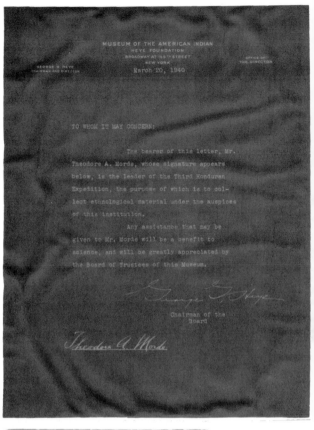

George Heye's letter of reference affirming Morde's role in the Third Honduran Expedition. *(Courtesy of Dave Morde)*

Morde's military identification. *(Courtesy of Dave Morde)*

Morde found a forty-foot pitpan to take him up the Rio Patuca. *(Courtesy of Dave Morde)*

At first, we tried to make a raft from scratch. *(Courtesy of the author)*

The roads weren't really roads. *(Courtesy of the author)*

Pancho's shirt always looked freshly ironed. *(Courtesy of the author)*

Pancho and Juan with the fragile Geo Prizm and the last of our water. *(Courtesy of the author)*

Chris Begley, real-life Indiana Jones. *(Courtesy of the author)*

The coffee was as sweet as pure sugarcane juice. *(Courtesy of the author)*

A woman, a girl, and a chicken appeared as if from thin air. *(Courtesy of the author)*

An old settler warned us of "a witch who protects the gold." *(Courtesy of the author)*

A Frog in the bow.
(Courtesy of the author)

Camp. *(Courtesy of the author)*

Every day we walked for miles and miles and miles. *(Courtesy of the author)*

The walls of a lost city perhaps? *(Courtesy of the author)*

What did Morde know that he wasn't writing? *(Courtesy of Dave Morde)*

In the Lost City of Ancient America's Monkey God

Explorer Theodore Morde Finds in Honduras Jungles a Vanished Civilization's Prehistoric Metropolis Where Sacrifices Were Made to the Gigantic Idol of an Ape—and Describes the Weird "Dance of the Dead Monkeys" Still Practiced by Natives in Whom Runs the Olden Blood

American Weekly boasted a circulation of 50 million— an exaggeration. *(American Weekly / Hearst)*

An artist's renderings of the Dance of the Dead
Monkeys and the Temple of the Monkey God.
(American Weekly/Hearst)

GATEWAY TO THE LOST CITIES

"**H**ERE WE ARE," said Chris as our speedboat bumped up the Río Wampú. "It's the gateway to the lost cities."

The protagonist of Paul Theroux's *The Mosquito Coast*, Allie Fox, made a similar voyage up a fictionalized Río Wampú with his wife and three kids. In pursuit of a happier, simpler life, far away from an America that he believed to be in decline, Fox and his family eventually settle on a sliver of land along the river. They build huts and plant gardens, and soon they hear rumors of an ancient tribe, untouched by civilization, deep in the forest. "The Munchies kept themselves hidden in secret cities in the jungle," a native tells Fox. "They had been here longer than the Miskito Indians, or Pech, or Tawahkas or Zambus. . . . They were tall and built pyramids and were in all respects a noble people." Fox goes in search of the tribe, wondering what true freedom from modern life looks like, but he never finds them.

We had paid a skinny Tawahka man named Jiménez $150 to take us up on a fifteen-foot tin boat with a forty-horsepower Yamaha engine that the Indian owner had said made it the "fastest boat on this part of the river." Three hours later, after we entered the rugged mountains, not far from the place on the map where Dr. Jesús

Aguilar Paz had inscribed his famous question mark for the White City, Jiménez slowed the boat and let out a whistle.

He steered into a claustrophobic branch off the river and shut down the engine, allowing the boat to glide into a muddy bank. For a minute I thought we were stopping to take stock of the damage the boat had suffered on the bumpy ride upstream. But then he pointed at the rising leafage in front of us. "It's here," he said. "The path."

There was no path, but we climbed out. When I joked that maybe he'd like to come with us, he was unamused. He restarted the engine and reversed the boat. We were again alone.

I began to strap on my shin guards but then decided it was too hot and my legs were too tired to walk with them on. Then something cracked overhead: a gang of monkeys in the trees. Suddenly fruit and pieces of wood were raining down on us. "They're attacking us!" Chris yelled. Ducking for cover, we unsheathed our machetes and headed for the lost city.

▼　▼　▼

WE HAD WALKED only about five minutes before Pancho raised his hand and a stranger stepped out of the green gloom. My first thought was that we were about to be ambushed. The man had shaggy black hair, clumped into greasy threads, and was hunched forward like a running back pushing through a line. His face was smudged with dirt; his jeans were slick with mud. He carried a satchel over his shoulder and swung a machete in one hand.

We never caught his name. He must have been in his late twenties or early thirties, though he had a boyish face, with murky eyes that looked like a churned-up tide pool. He said he lived in a village east of there and had been walking since the sun came up. Chris asked where he was going, and a flash of recognition crossed his face.

"My son is very sick," the man said. "I am going to see him in Catacamas"—a two- or three-day walk. He looked up into the heavy canopy of trees, as if searching for light. There was none, only shade.

The man stuck his machete into the mud and leaned on it. Then he told us a story, taking deep breaths, as if he were slowly being unburdened of a great weight. "My baby boy was born, and he was healthy then," he said. That had been about a month before. But then his boy had fallen ill, and his tiny body had become very hot. "*Caliente*," he said, pointing at his forehead.

Over this rough land, through rivers and swamps and mountain, he and his wife had carried the newborn to a medical clinic in Catacamas, where a doctor had diagnosed a strain of flu. After a couple weeks, the baby had seemed to improve and the man had returned to his village, leaving behind his wife and baby to stay with the doctor.

A few weeks had passed, and then, a day ago, his wife had sent him a message on the radio. "She said that our son is very sick again. She said that I must come quickly." He moved his hands in front of his narrow body, trying to make sense of something that lacked cause. Biting his lip, he said, "I'm worried that he is going to die."

That was the last he said. He turned to go, and we followed him for a while up a steep streambed, where mud rose to our knees. He moved faster and faster, pulling farther ahead of our group, and after about an hour he was gone.

"THEY HAD ORDERS TO SHOOT"

I **LOOKED OUT THE** back window a few times," Morde wrote of the car ride to rendezvous with the German ambassador.

Worried that he was being followed by rival spies who also wanted to see the enemy, he instructed the driver to go at a fast pace through Istanbul before turning onto a back road and then racing again. He kept his head craned backward, but there was no one that he could see.

Morde carried with him a small translucent sheet of gelatin, outlining in tiny print his secret operation to kill or capture Hitler. It was unreadable without a magnifying glass. At the edge of the city, the car jerked to a halt in front of the German embassy. As he climbed out, Morde suspiciously eyed a man sitting in a car on the opposite side of the street—who was that?—and then hurried through the gate.

Inside, a bodyguard led him to a study with views of the Bosporus Strait and the walls featuring one notable decoration: a life-size portrait of Hitler in Nazi uniform. As he recalled in his official report, which would be declassified many years later, Morde was now behind enemy lines.

At the time, von Papen was considered one of Germany's most

prominent political figures, not to mention something of an enigma—the press described him as "a slick silver fox." In 1932, under President Paul von Hindenburg, von Papen had served as the chancellor of Germany. Years earlier, during World War I, he had been expelled from the United States for organizing several bombings in New Jersey. When Hitler took power, von Papen was seen as a rival to the Nazi leader. He was demoted to vice chancellor and then to the rank of diplomat. In that role he had aided in the Nazi annexation of Austria. In the infamous purge of the summer of 1934 known as the Night of the Long Knives, the Nazi regime executed many of von Papen's allies; hundreds of people were murdered. Von Papen was spared, however. And though he eventually returned to Hitler's inner circle ("We must never part until our work is accomplished," Hitler once said to him), he sometimes felt like a dead man walking.

"I came as a trusted messenger," Morde told the ambassador, explaining that he was "disguised" as a journalist. His presence in Istanbul was "an absolute secret" and he hadn't checked in with any authorities.

"Mr. Mord-a," said the ambassador with a heavy German accent.

In photographs, von Papen's lined face gave nothing away—his high flat forehead, stiff brushed mustache, and cold slits for eyes. The smile, patient and empty, could have been that of an executioner.

"A man in my position has a great weight to carry and many troubles," the ambassador told Morde. "Several attempts have been made on my life." The last close call had come a year earlier, when the Soviets had tried to bomb him.

Instinctually, von Papen would consider Morde an adversary. If his visit was not some kind of U.S. trick, perhaps Morde was a gestapo agent assigned to execute him.

Von Papen offered Morde a Turkish cigarette, and the two men sat down and smoked. Following a bit of light talk, though, Morde felt that the ambassador "no longer entertained any suspicions."

They were free to talk. So he reached into his pocket and produced the secret document. "It contains something you might finding interesting," he told von Papen. "You only have my word to vouch for whether this represents any one's true opinions or not."

As the ambassador read the document through a magnifying glass, Morde was struck by the emotion that suddenly washed over the man's face. "It seemed to me that tears were very close to his eyes," he wrote, surely relieved.

Seeing his opening, Morde laid out the plot for ending the war. With his heart pounding, he said it was time for the Germans to "get rid of Hitler" and that the Allied bombing would not end until the führer's "capture or his death."

Morde told him that his plan involved building up a group of German allies inside the country who would eventually rise up and, at the right moment, grab Hitler. He wanted von Papen to head up the operation, from recruiting the necessary people inside Germany to making sure that the plot went according to plan. Once captured, Morde said, the German dictator "could be flown out of Germany to a spot under American control."

Von Papen nodded, his eyes locked with Morde's.

And then the ambassador spoke. If the United States had Hitler, he wondered, what would it do with him? "Would he be treated as a prisoner of war?"

Morde didn't know, but he suspected that he would be "treated . . . in accordance with his former rank as head of a state and confined in a safe place."

The ambassador said that he would need time to think. As Morde stood to leave, von Papen placed a hand on the explorer's shoulder and leaned close to his ear. "You cannot realize how seriously affected I am by this talk." It was an utterly unexpected sentiment. Pointing at a vehicle out front, he added, a bit cryptically, "The car has men in it whose job is to protect me. If you had made an attempt against my life, they had orders to shoot."

▼ ▼ ▼

THAT NIGHT MORDE returned to a safe house, where he waited for von Papen to think things through.

In that business, there was a lot of waiting, and during those times the lost city occasionally entered his thoughts—the remoteness of the place, the serenity of the jungle gloom in its green profusion, the Westerners on the rivers who had left behind the warring world where he now made his way.

What had become of Camp Ulak? And what had happened to Burke? What about the German banana runners? The Tawahka Indians?

As the years passed, he worried that someone else might find his city. He needed to get back. He kept an eye on the news, watching for other expeditions. Meanwhile, he had heard that his friend Laurence Brown was also getting sucked into the terrible war.

In the first of three letters to the Explorers Club, he wrote, "It is my intention to return to the field of exploration as soon as the world conditions permit. Much remains to be done in Honduras."

Still, even as he reminisced about the ancient place and talked about returning, the life of a spy increasingly engulfed him. The thing was, to be anything but single-minded in the midst of war was to risk death.

MY LOWEST LOW

NIGHTFALL CAME, AND we were still climbing the mountain. The man's story had left all of us silent, churning it over in our heads, until at last Pancho bent down and pointed at paw prints in the mud. "Jaguar," he said. It seemed we were being followed. The heat had sucked out my energy, and I was lagging behind. Then people started to disappear. First I lost sight of Pancho and then of Angel. Soon Chris vanished too.

I paused for a minute and began to laugh hysterically because I was suddenly alone in this shithole jungle, as if everything had been headed for this particular moment.

Trying not to panic, I walked on and spent a long time slogging through ankle-deep muck, imagining that eventually I would find them. I made good progress for some time, trying to feel positive and hopeful about moving forward without falling on my face. But before I knew it I was treading through ten-foot-high razor grass that shut out the world, and every time I thought the grass would end, it kept going. I slipped and fell, water and sludge filling my boots and pants. I cut my hand on a rock. My shirt ripped at the chest. Mosquitoes had turned my skin to blood, and my new beard itched. I tried to jump a mud hole but tripped and fell into it instead.

That's when I stopped. I slumped down under a tall mahogany

tree and called out to Chris. To Pancho. To Angel. "Hello!" The siren pulse of insects swallowed up my voice. There was no echo. No one answered. I was out of breath. I was too tired to walk anymore. I couldn't feel my legs. My eyelids were stones.

Sitting in the mud, I couldn't get that young man's face out of my head, how he was racing to see his dying son. He would probably not see his son live to be a year old—and I had just missed my daughter's fourth birthday. I remembered the dead man I'd seen on the road weeks back. The aggressive loneliness of the place weighed on me. I was risking my life—the pirates, the snakes, the malarial air, the stalking jaguar—and for what? I remembered something Amy had said to me once: "We need to make memories together."

My emotions bent out of shape. The farther I went into the jungle, the farther my family seemed to slip away. They were getting along without me. What had I done? In my notebook, I flipped to an open page and scribbled, "I'm so far gone," while I began to laugh, and cry.

"I'M HAVING THE TIME OF MY LIFE"

VON PAPEN CALLED for a meeting the morning after they met and directed Morde to a private house on Prinkipo Island in the Sea of Marmara, an hour's boat ride from the mainland. When the spy arrived, the ambassador was alone. He said that he had taken his own boat to avoid being trailed. The night before, von Papen had spent hours preparing his thoughts, writing them down on three single-spaced pages that he said he intended to destroy after the meeting.

Take notes, he told Morde, but "you are to show them to no one other than the President."

Then the ambassador's words came out in a rush, as if a pause might cause second thoughts. "Americans seem to think all Germans are Nazis," he said, according to Morde's official report. "That is not true."

If anything was to be done about ending this war, von Papen said, he would require assurances. Morde's plan called for building a counterrevolutionary force, but von Papen said his "friends" would not commit to doing that without a guarantee of peace for Germany, as well as a leadership role for it in Europe after the war.

Regarding Morde's endgame of extracting Hitler, von Papen said that there was one potential obstacle: "the Nazis were still capable of

tricks." In carrying out the plan, von Papen worried, his life, as well
as the lives of his family, would be in danger.

But would he do it? Morde wanted to know. "Are you willing to
do your utmost to get rid of Hitler?"

Morde watched him move forward in his chair. "Yes," the ambassador said at last. "Tell your President I will leave to contact my
people in Germany. Tell him I must have something definite to offer
them. Tell him that I will do my best."

To stay in touch, the ambassador gave Morde a secret code to
decipher telegrams. They had to be very cautious. "[Von Papen]
said that he trusted me, and that I must be very careful," Morde explained in a top secret agency wire. "And that in turn I could trust
him without reservation not to disclose what took place between
us." When Morde turned to go, the ambassador wished him luck,
and the men agreed to talk again in five or six weeks.

▼ ▼ ▼

DAYS LATER, A military plane whisked Morde to Washington,
where controversy immediately erupted. The plan caused a feud
between Roosevelt's two most trusted spy chiefs.

Robert Sherwood, who was the head of the Office of War Information, urged the president to reject the plot and even denied the
government's role in it. He suggested that Morde was operating as a
rogue agent and "making a certain amount of trouble."

Wild Bill Donovan, Morde's immediate boss, however, encouraged Roosevelt to consider the plan as a possible way to end the war.
"I beg you to read this carefully," he wrote to the president in a top
secret memo. "It contains an idea that your skill and imagination
could develop. . . . If the plan went through, and if the culprits were
delivered and fittingly tried and executed, and if the unconditional
surrender resulted, it would strengthen your position morally at the
peace table."

Without ever meeting Morde, Roosevelt rebuffed the plan; although he never explained why, the sense was that such a single-
handed clandestine scheme would disrupt the tenuous alliance with

Stalin and potentially undermine the Allied agreement to seek an unconditional surrender, which included the total annihilation of the Nazis and the war machine that they had created.

Of course, people would later wonder what the world would have looked like if Hitler had been murdered then. Millions of lives might have been saved, but the act might have also turned Russia against the United States, creating an entirely new front in the war.

One mystery that would remain is who actually initiated the Istanbul plot—the OSS or Morde himself? Donovan would never say, and neither would Morde.

As for the ambassador, Morde didn't see him again. "Two or three messages did come through from Papen to Morde, which we could not break," recalled John Toulmin, the head of the OSS branch in Cairo. "We have no idea what they said." How much recruiting von Papen did for the internal capture-or-kill group, no one will ever know.

Later, U.S. troops would seize the ambassador in Germany. According to one of the soldiers with him that day, von Papen was overheard mumbling, "I wish this terrible war were over." Following the Allied victory, von Papen would be tried at Nuremberg and acquitted.

Morde, meanwhile, was transferred to the Maritime Unit of the OSS, where he spent the rest of the conflict.

▼ ▼ ▼

"I'M ON THE wagon," he wrote in a report from Livorno, Italy, not far from Genoa on the Ligurian Sea. He had begun drinking recently but now decided it was time to wind it down for fear it was turning him upside down.

Livorno had been wrecked by the war. Bridges were out, the roads full of ruts; the harbor was a graveyard of sunken ships, the coast a minefield waiting to explode.

As in the jungle, it rained a lot, and Morde's existence there was a rugged hell. "We lay down on a pile of rubble on a chewed-up pier. . . . Half the men are down with colds," he wrote one week.

The air stank of smoke. He spent a lot time on the sea, where his wandering life had started. In Maritime Intelligence (MI), he headed up an eighty-five-foot patrol boat that chased submarines, inserted agents behind enemy lines, planted mines underwater, collected naval intelligence, and engaged in amphibious sabotage. By 1945, Morde was an OSS chief.

Occasionally, his mind drifted to life back in the States and what it might actually be like to have a place he could, for once, call home. In a letter that winter to the Explorers Club, he wrote, "The war has provided me with many fine experiences, including an opportunity to complete another trip (during the past fourteen months) around the world. One doesn't get any younger, however, and I look forward with pleasure to a few months of settled existence in the U.S."

Still, while other agents complained about their uncomfortable bases, the wandering, the bad weather, the constant danger, Morde mostly seemed to relish the adventure at hand. One year, he wrote in a memo to the Washington bureau, "I'm having the time of my life."

▼ ▼ ▼

FOR HIS FINAL assignment, in July 1945, he headed for the Japanese-held island of Weichow, twenty-three miles south of the Gulf of Tonkin. It was the rainy season. As he and his two men fought high seas on a small fishing boat, they suddenly encountered twenty-four Japanese junks that opened fire on them.

He probably should have retreated but instead fought back for two days. Eventually, a thick fog provided him with enough cover to slip past the enemy line and onto the island. The men made camp and went off in different directions, scouting the land for intelligence. But when Morde returned to camp, after clearing debris from a runway so U.S. Army Air Forces planes could land, he found one of his men beheaded. It was an ambush. With the Japanese opening fire, the men scrambled to their boat and the man beside Morde was shot in half.

For his efforts, Morde was awarded the Bronze Star. But the violence would haunt him. After World War II ended, he resigned from the OSS, noting in a classified memo that he had taken "no sick leave."

In a final letter to the secretary of the Explorers Club, Donald B. Upham, in the winter of 1945, Morde recalled his five years of duty overseas and, with a note of fatigue, said that his future plans were now up in the air. He didn't know what he was going to do next. "There will come a day when I hope to be able to visit you frequently," he wrote to Upham, somewhat dreamily, seeming to imply that he desired to visit with other explorers there and figure out a way to return to his lost city. "It is possible that I will take part once more in the world of exploration, but it is too early to decide at present."

JOURNEY TO THE CROSSES

THE VOICE SAVED me.

"You okay?" It was Chris. He had doubled back. I looked at him. How much time had passed was hard to say. His face was a mess of mud, and his glasses were fogged.

"I hate this," I said and enumerated. I hated the walking. I hated the Clif Bars. I hated the beans and rice. I hated my two sets of clothes. I hated carrying my backpack. I hated Pancho's radio that gave us only bad news about the coup and dead people. I hated the acrid iodine-infused water. I hated the malarial fog in my head. I hated the jungle. I hated the goddamn lost city.

Chris nodded. "I know. It's rough."

I felt an urge to punch him.

I stood up, and for a moment we remained there. Angel and Pancho had returned. Chris had been telling Pancho we were headed in the wrong direction, and finally Pancho had figured out that we had been circling the mountain for hours instead of climbing it.

"We have to keep moving," Chris said now. "It's getting dark."

I took a deep breath, closed my eyes, trying to suppress the hate, and forced myself to go on. We slogged for another five or six hours through miles of up-and-down muddiness, keeping an eye out, as ever, for snakes and jaguars.

Night came. At one point I begged to stop, but Pancho began worrying about bandits.

Feeling the hate coming back again, I tried to imagine myself somewhere else—on a beach or a lake or just on the couch at home, comfortable, settled, living a conventional life. But the jungle kept intruding, like an enemy that won't let you go even when you are dying and long past saving. On one steep descent through a canyon, my pant leg snagged on a tree trunk and ripped up the seam. I nearly lost my pants. Two minutes later, I stepped into a bog and toppled over. I had warm mud in my nose, mouth, down my underwear, up my shirt, dripping from my beard, my hair. I felt the smooth carapace of a sizable insect and tasted bug. Standing, I took two more steps and fell again, the hate pouring back into me.

"You gonna make it?" Chris yelled.

The mud had by now infiltrated every pore of my body. I had nothing left inside me. I couldn't laugh or cry if I wanted to. I didn't think I could move.

Then I felt something on my neck. It was Pancho, in his perfectly pressed blue button-down shirt, his hand lifting me out.

I don't really know how I made it. I wrapped a piece of string around my leg to keep my ripped pants together and went on. For an hour or so Pancho had been claiming that he heard dogs, suggesting a settlement, but I didn't hear anything and thought he was just trying to give me hope. But he was right. Eventually, we came to a tiny village called Cielo Azul, or Blue Sky.

The village of some half-dozen huts straddled a valley. At the first one, a Ladino man in his fifties, with his sombrero tilted forward on his head and a pistol on his belt, invited us in to eat. "You are welcome," he said. I thought I was dreaming.

▼ ▼ ▼

HIS WIFE SERVED us the usual, and we ate the beans on a crude wood bench outside. Somehow Pancho had found batteries for his radio, and news of the coup filled the damp night air; little had changed. The death toll had risen to seven, and there were new rumors that younger officers in the military might rebel against the coup leader. I tuned the news out. I was grateful to be at rest and grateful to be alive. Even the beans were okay.

Above us the stars were bright and close, the moon's giant whiteness flooding the valley. The air smelled of pine. The owner of the hut asked where we were going. No Americans had ever passed through here. When Chris pointed west, the man said, "Las Crucitas," the Crosses. He said the area was considered a burial ground. "We don't go there," his wife said. She had emerged from the hut and now stood beside him in a white dress and flip-flops. "Strange things go on there," she said.

Other people from the village began to appear, drawn in by our voices echoing in the night. "There are many large mounds around there. Tall as that," the owner of the hut said, pointing at a thirty-foot palm tree next to us.

Another man, with a handlebar mustache and muscular shoulders, materialized from the shadows. "The ones who lived there were giants. The giants built those mounds," he said. "Who else could move those big rocks? Have you seen the pottery scattered out there? It's huge." All eyes were on him, the butt of a 9-millimeter jutting from his dirty white jeans.

He suggested that the giants were buried in the hills and made a rocketing gesture at the midnight stars. "There are green lights that shoot up from the mounds. We see them sometimes. The lights go up, and then they are gone."

That night we slept in our hammocks next to a stream. Because there was an open pasture nearby, I managed to get a signal on the satellite phone. My daughter picked up, and her small voice sent my mind back to my agony hours before. I told her how sorry I was that I'd missed her birthday, how sorry I was to be away, that it had been so long since I'd seen her, that I thought about her every day and wished I was home with her. I was so happy to hear her voice. But she didn't want to talk about any of that.

"Have you seen any snakes?" she asked, cutting me off.

I said I had.

"Are they scary, Daddy? What do they look like? Are they slip-pery?"

I told her that I'd seen an orange one and that sometimes they scared me.

"Have you seen Curious George?" she asked.

Amy came on. The first thing that came out of my mouth was "Did the raccoon come back?"

She said it hadn't, but she didn't sleep in our room anymore. She had duct-taped the window, and the woman upstairs had helped her screw a slatted steel window guard into place. At night she left the lights on. "I'm sleeping on a blow-up mattress in Sky's room," she said. "I'm tired."

I began to apologize to her too, but she cut me off. "Listen," she said, "we've been worried about you."

We had been at odds about this trip, and now it sounded as though she had gone through her own process of thinking.

"Are you okay?" she asked.

I tried to tell her everything that had happened, but there was no time. "It's just good to hear your voice," she said. We spoke for about ten minutes, and then I told her I was coming home. "We miss you," she said.

"FROM JOURNALIST AND EXPLORER AND SPY TO A FATHER"

WHY DIDN'T THEODORE MORDE ever go back to the lost city? How did his life come apart? Did he die by his own hand, or was one of his enemies taking revenge? It's impossible to answer those questions. What's certain is that his life was turned upside down when he met a girl at a New York City party in the summer of 1948.

Gloria Gustafson was a model: blond, leggy, with a sparkling white smile that "turned heads," as Morde told his family. She was twenty-two and had been staying at the Barbizon Hotel for Women at the corner of Lexington Avenue and Sixty-third Street. A kind of finishing school, it was home to countless fashionable young women over the years, from Grace Kelly to Joan Crawford and Edith Bouvier Beale.

Morde had taken a "consulting" job in 1947 with the Egyptian president, Gamal Abdel Nasser, which may or may not have been an informal intelligence mission. The last year had brought him writing assignments and radio shows, and, later, when the Arab-Israeli conflict erupted in the late 1940s, he made a twenty-eight-minute black-and-white documentary of the Gaza strip, *Sands of Sorrow*, about the suffering in Palestinian refugee camps.

What the two talked about at the party in Manhattan is lost to time, as is much of their short life together. Family members remember, though, that Morde fell for Gustafson almost immediately—something that hadn't happened to him before. He had spent his life running away to far-flung parts of the world, and it seemed as though he'd forgotten about love or that love had forgotten about him. But she drew him in, and he kept looking at her. He liked the fact that every man in the room was gawking at her slender figure and her lipsticked smile. "I'm visiting some friends in the Hamptons over the weekend," he had said, according to family. "Do you want to come?"

Maybe she laughed and turned a little red in the face, maybe she looked down at her feet or off across the crowded room of revelers. Maybe she just broke the news: she couldn't come, she was about to marry another man.

But that didn't stop Morde. He was ardent. He pleaded with her to give him a chance.

"You don't get it, do you?" she likely said. "I'm getting married."

Morde favored bespoke suits and ties knotted tight to his neck, and he seemed to know everyone who mattered. That's what Gustafson would remember, according to family. Over the years, when he returned to Manhattan, he had become recognizable among New York's society circles. He was a regular on sailing trips with the Vanderbilts. Some would say it had been his job as a spy to mingle in society circles and he just kept it up after the war. It was a natural fit for a hero who knew how to tell a good story. Maybe that's why Gustafson ultimately changed her mind: she sensed that the man standing in front of her was different from all the others who had tried to seduce her over the years. "I'll go," she said. What the hell.

Three weeks later, on August 11, they were married—but not before Morde warned Gustafson about his wanderlust. "Look," he might have said, "I have an unusual lifestyle. I travel—a lot."

Gustafson surely grinned. She had done her fair share of traveling as a model. "Okay with me! What are we waiting for?"

They traveled to Europe, Africa, and the Middle East, where

Morde introduced her to some of his old life. They spent some time in Washington, D.C., and made at least two boat trips from New York to the Egyptian coastal city of Alexandria. At one point, they lived on a seventy-foot double-masted wooden sailboat, moored along the Nile River. Morde did some freelance writing, a mixture of hard foreign reporting and softer travelogues.

Then he became a father. Christine was born in the spring of 1951 and Teddy two years later. Gustafson stopped modeling and gave herself over to motherhood. They returned to the United States and lived for a time in Alexandria, Virginia, in a house with a view of the Potomac River, and then settled down in a one-story brick waterfront house in Stamford, Connecticut. Morde's downfall came soon after.

▼ ▼ ▼

ONCE THE FAMILY moved to Connecticut, Morde stopped traveling so much. It reminded me of when my family picked up everything and moved from Manhattan to sleepy Brooklyn. It was jarring. Amy and I were scared. We painted the walls, bought new furniture, put up pictures—a way of settling in, trying to make the place our own. The first few months we walked around the five rooms, marveling at how much more space we had. We sat in the living room at night with the windows wide open and couldn't believe the quiet. When we had been living in the East Village, the streets had been so loud all night we'd had to shut the windows to sleep. The quiet was our new world.

In 1952, likely feeling the pressures to provide for his new family, Morde did the unthinkable. At forty-one years old, for the first time in his life, he accepted a true nine-to-five office job—as the head of the recently launched television division at the Associated Press. For most people, such a job would have been the start of the prime of life, when the future crystallizes and prosperity is suddenly within reach. Not so for Morde. "The last few years of his life were a downward spiral," his grandson Joseph Essaye III told me. Gustafson wouldn't talk to me about Morde, but Essaye spoke to his grandmother for me. "He went from journalist and explorer and spy to a father. That was very hard on him," Essaye recalled. I said I understood. Adulthood seems a great compromise.

For Gustafson and Morde, the honeymoon was over. The couple argued, and it didn't help that she didn't get along very well with his mother, according to his extended family. There were days when husband and wife hardly spoke. Their marriage was crumbling.

The disappointments compounded the troubles. When he lost out on a top news job at CBS in New York, Dave Morde told me, he blamed it on his documentary *Sands of Sorrow*, which had received some negative press for its controversial embrace of the Palestinians. He grew taciturn with friends and loved ones, as though his mind was somewhere else, and he spent much of his free time alone.

Some days, when he wasn't working at the Associated Press, he walked down to Seaview Harbor, rigged up his sailboat, and steered it into Long Island Sound. It was a gorgeous boat about fifty feet long, black as onyx, with two towering masts. Once out, there was nothing like the open water. That was freedom—the feeling that you could point the boat toward the distant horizon and keep going, as he had done when he'd stowed away on that steamship when he was a teenager. On the water, away from his screaming kids, the salty wind blowing against his cleanly shaved face, Morde had time to think. What had happened to his life? Where had he made a wrong turn? Could he really be one of those people who settle down?

▼ ▼ ▼

ALL ALONG HE continued to dwell on the Lost City of the Monkey God. More than a decade had passed since his expedition to Honduras, and it was getting increasingly hard to summon up the more intimate memories. According to some family members, he grew concerned that people doubted his discovery. If he had found something as amazing as he'd described, why hadn't he returned? What was he hiding?

But Morde, as the years passed, simply couldn't return. He was a different person, with a family and a job he couldn't leave behind to spend months in the jungle. He had bills to pay, a household to keep afloat. He was trying to stay focused, according to family, to keep his life on track, to be a good husband and a good father to his children, a common struggle. But it was not a struggle that came naturally to Morde—or one that would find a happy resolution.

It was sometime around 1953 that he finally confronted Gustafson about all of it. "I can't do this right now," he told her, according to family. "I have to go." There was talk of separation. He was drinking heavily again, a habit that was anathema to his Christian Scientist mother. Whatever mystery he owned about his life, both lived and unlived, whatever regrets or secrets he kept, curdled deeper inside of him.

Eventually he moved out and stayed at his parents' summerhouse in Dartmouth, Massachusetts. His mother and father had recently moved to Florida, selling his childhood home in New Bedford. But he was in Dartmouth only briefly before he departed again, a decision that seemed to baffle his father, who couldn't keep track of his son.

In December 1953, Albert Morde wrote to the Explorers Club: "It is uncertain at this writing as to what [Theodore's] next address will be. . . . You had better [write] him at my address here, and I will take care of the forwarding of your notices and letters, same as I did over a period of years past. Then if and when he again gets an address to which you should send mail, I will let you know."

▾ ▾ ▾

AMID THE DARKNESS, Morde's mind regularly drifted back to the war years, stirring up demons that he'd rather forget. "He believed that someone from his days in the OSS was pursuing him," his niece Susan Shumway told me. "He became very paranoid about that." At another time, she added, "I think he may have been questioning everything. . . . What was really important? For example, the deaths of people he knew, possibly deaths he felt responsible for. War can do that."

Joan Cenedella, another niece, said it was impossible to know much of anything about him during these final years. He was closed up. "It was difficult to ever know what he was going to do," she said. "He was sophisticated and handsome, but he was a mystery."

Shumway agreed. "That is very much how I remember Ted. Handsome, debonair, distant."

By the summer of 1954, it seemed clear that Morde's marriage to Gustafson was over for good. No one remembers the exact date. But Morde returned to Stamford, packed his family into his black Oldsmobile sedan, and drove them to Gustafson's family's house in Rhode Island. It was there that he said good-bye. At the time his children were one and three years old. Later, Morde's family would say that there was no indication that that good-bye was meant to be forever. He said it as though he would see everyone again soon; he just needed some time to think and figure things out.

But on June 26, he was back in Dartmouth at his parents' house, where his brother, Elton, found him at 3:30 p.m., suspended in the shower stall, naked except for his bathrobe, a thick rope looped around his neck. There was no saving him. Theodore Ambrose Morde was forty-three years old.

▾ ▾ ▾

HIS DEATH CAME as a complete shock. His family would never know what to make of it. He was not a deeply depressive person and had never spoken of suicide. "I want to believe it was a rival spy," his nephew Dave Morde told me. "It just doesn't make sense otherwise." Others would suppose that the lost-city spirits had killed him. He had seen the city, they thought, and he would pay the price with his soul. "I know that my grandmother—Ted's mother—once told me that the natives in Honduras believed the site he found was cursed and that he had violated this curse by going there," Shumway said.

Two days after his death, the *New York Times* published an obituary, remembering the man who had "explored the ruins of ancient Indian civilization." He was buried at the Rural Cemetery in

New Bedford, the city where he had been born and where he had watched the whaling ships go off to sea.

On June 29, the secretary of the Explorers Club mailed a letter of condolence to the Morde family, describing their son and brother as a "true explorer. Both you and the Club have every reason to be proud of Theodore." Albert Morde must not have seen the letter. Three days later, he composed a short note to the club—it was four sentences—notifying them of his son's death. He asked that a note of it go into its records, and, as if he wanted to put those days to rest, he requested that they "kindly stop all mail for him from now on."

In the intervening decades, Gustafson would remarry and, according to family, try to forget some of those times she had spent with Theodore Morde. For her, I was told that it was impossible to reconcile the adventurous, loving man she had met that summer day in Manhattan in 1948 with the man who had abandoned her almost six years later. According to her grandson, Joseph Essaye, she never forgave his decision to leave her and their young children. Today Gustafson lives on the east coast of Florida, but she doesn't talk much about any of it, according to family.

As for the lost city, the legend became a casualty of time. Morde's notebooks detailing his Honduran expedition gathered dust, were misplaced, and, for a while, went missing. Perhaps they got lost when the Museum of the American Indian was sold to the Smithsonian or when George Heye died in 1957. One journal was said to have burned in a fire. The walking stick disappeared for some time too, which was a fitting end for a man who seemed determined to protect his sacred discovery.

After Morde was gone, the only living person with knowledge of what he had found and where he found it was his old expedition partner Laurence Brown. Whether the two friends saw each other again after the war or if Brown was present at Morde's funeral, no one knows. Brown died in 1974 without adding anything more to the story of the lost city.

THE MORDE THEORY

WE WALKED FOR hours in the blazing sun before we found the ruins. It was August 1, about a month from the day I had arrived in Honduras. Around us, the forest alternated with land that had been burned and cut, where copper-red shapes of mahogany stumps stood out of islands of second-growth grass and vines. The bandits had captured Chris close to this area, but we didn't talk about that.

Steadily, we pushed forward. We had paid a man from Blue Sky to come along with us. He had a pistol pushed into his belt and a rifle on the mule that high-stepped through the brush. We saw the large mounds that the settlers had mentioned the night before. Some as high as ten feet and in groupings of twos and threes, they were larger than the mounds we'd spotted along the river. "They're everywhere!" exclaimed Chris, a bit stunned. I couldn't stop thinking about the entombed giants, and I had the feeling I was walking through a graveyard. Pancho, who had been quiet most of the way, started to complain of stomach pains and blamed it on the evil mountain spirits. "We must be getting close to the city," he said.

Soon Chris paused in a stand of tall trees. "Look there," he said, flicking his machete at the shaded ground. "It's easy to miss." He kicked away some vines, revealing disfigured cobblestones scattered about in what resembled a crude pathway. "It's a road," he said excitedly.

"A road?" I repeated, imagining asphalt with yellow broken lines.

"Yeah, a road. It's probably a thousand years old or more."

He said that roads had been built between neighboring cities and from city centers to the closest river, where people and goods were shipped into and out of the jungle. "You couldn't move here without a road. Think of all that mud we walked through."

Chris scrambled ahead until he stopped again at an open expanse where two large stone walls protruded from the grassy earth. Several feet tall, rounded off at the top, with decades of creepers and weeds engorging them, the walls extended for many yards, like giant serpents, before disappearing into the horizon. It reminded me of Morde's notes: "We found . . . walls upon which the green of the jungle had worked small damages."

"Do you see it?" Chris asked now. He pointed across the upturned carpet of green wilderness. It was early afternoon. For the first time in days there weren't any dark clouds in the sky. But the rain would come. It always did.

"What?" I asked.

He smiled. "The city," he said.

"What city?" I didn't see anything. Of course, I had been imagining great ruined white buildings, tall vine-strangled columns, spooky statues of giant monkey kings.

Chris chuckled. "You're standing on it," he said. "It's all over."

▼ ▼ ▼

THE GREAT LOST city sprawled across the jagged mountainside and along the Río Aner that rushed through the valley below. In Morde's notes about his discovery, he wrote of "towering mountains . . . providing a backdrop to the scene" and "a rushing cataract." He also noted that the ruins were "blanketed in centuries of growth." We stumbled up and down, surveying the contours of the ground, the nubs of grass, and the rock formations. Chris noticed lots of things that I didn't see. He pointed out clusters of twelve-foot-high man-made mounds—neighborhoods of the city's elites or govern-ment buildings. There were more walls, where other structures would have been erected, more roads and open plazas. "This was once a big city," he said.

At one point, he leaned over the face of a blackened boulder the size of a truck tire, which was etched with curious markings—dots, lines, squiggles, faces. "It's a petroglyph," he said.

"Does it mean anything?"

One arrow looked as though it was entering a body. I thought I saw a sun and a happy face.

Chris shook his head. "It could mean many things," he said. He had lately begun using 3D technology to analyze the tiny eroded images on the stones, but he and his colleagues in the archaeologi-cal community were still a long way from any real understanding of language and meaning. The carvings, he said, could be astrological maps or directions to an important religious place, a route to the underworld or even to another city. They could also have been sha-manic messages to the spirits. "We just don't know," he said.

I was going crazy inside. What was this place? "So is this Morde's Lost City of the Monkey God?" I asked. In the distance I could hear the howler monkeys—Morde had worried about "monkey faces [that] peered inquisitively" in the forest. Pancho and Angel had lagged behind with the gunman, who kept looking over his shoulder, as if he was expecting company. When Pancho had said, "I can feel the mountain spirits here," moments before, he had been only half joking.

Chris kept climbing. Near the top of the mountain, I noticed a dramatic pyramid-like rise in the earth, unlike any of the other man-made outcroppings we'd seen on our journey. It was blanketed in razor grass and trees—about four stories tall and as long as a football field. "This is amazing," said Chris. It was a temple.

We stood in front of it for a long time, taking it in, the way you might stand frozen beside a found spaceship, not knowing what to do next. There were more mounds rising underneath us and around us, and slowly I began to see it. The city seemed to begin and end here, the nexus of this civilization. "These people laid out their cities in very complicated, symbolic ways," Chris said. He said that the settlement had been built with beauty in mind but also with a sense of a specific cosmology, suggesting a more sophisticated civilization than the Spanish conquistadors had ever imagined. "They were more advanced than you'd think," he added.

He said that the city represented a kind of microcosm of their living universe—the upper world, the middle world, and the underworld. "The temple is the connection to the upper world," he said. "The plaza"—he made a gesture at the overgrown field where we were standing—"is the middle world, or our world."

"What about the underworld?" I asked.

"Maybe there was a cave somewhere or something built under the river. Or there could have been some sort of substructure at the south end of the plaza." (In many traditions in Mesoamerica, south symbolized down, while north was up.)

We trudged up the side of the temple. "You can see why they picked this place," said Chris, waving his hand at the view. Miles of forest unfolded in front of us, dropping into the river and then rising up another mountainside, where the pockmarked land suggested more ruins. It did seem perfect, I thought. This had to be it.

"That assumption that there was little in the Mosquitia, that this was always pristine rain forest, uninhabited," Chris said now, "you can see how that's just wrong." He seemed to take particular pleasure in the evidence undermining all the people who had challenged him over the years, those who had warned him he was wasting his time in the Mosquitia. Those people and their tired old arguments against a city ever existing in this rain forest. "Just look at this place!" he exclaimed.

I wanted to cry again, so many intense emotions were boiling up inside me. My knees wobbled.

Chris guessed that the greater city had been occupied sometime between AD 1000 and 1500 and that thousands of people, ancestors of the Tawahkas and Pech, had lived there. "This was probably the capital," he said. "All those small villages we passed—the mounds— were politically connected to this one."

"So what happened to the city?" I asked. Chris shrugged. He said a mass plague might have killed off the inhabitants. Or maybe there had been a war with a neighboring civilization. Or maybe they had died away slowly as the land or climate changed around them and the ones who remained abandoned the city. "It's hard to know for certain," he said. In his book *Collapse*, the scientist Jared Diamond argued that civilizations break down, fall into war, and end due largely to environmental issues, from deforestation and overfishing to soil loss and climate change. "A society's steep decline may begin only a decade or two after the society reaches its peak numbers, wealth and power," he wrote.

"A ghost town," I said, thinking of cities in the U.S. Midwest that had been left behind, the houses falling apart, the town centers in various states of decay.

In my mind, I could see Morde standing where I now stood: his overgrown beard, his emaciated body, the torn pants, the ruined boots. I thought of the extreme fatigue he must have felt during those four months in the wild, and then the awe and bliss of discovery at stumbling upon something that had been lost for so long. The romance of it.

I couldn't take it anymore. I asked again, "Is this the city Morde found?"

Chris looked up at the sky, which was now turning dark with rain. He didn't answer in a straightforward way. "I have a theory," he said. "Do you want to hear it?

▾ ▾ ▾

"I BET MORDE came up the Patuca hearing stories about the lost city and also working from what he knew from Heye and Captain Murray. He asked everyone about the city until someone offered to help. We know he was probably a very convincing man. Of course, he was probably very lucky too, because other people had gone searching for the city. But let's say he did get lucky.

"The first problem is time," he said. "When on that calendar of his did he actually make his discovery? Because he never mentions the discovery on the calendar, and yet most of his time is accounted for."

"The calendar was a red herring," I suggested.

"Right," he said. "It could have been off by a day or two. And in that time, he could have staged a trip from Ulak. But I bet he came here on his way home."

"Why?"

"He said in his notes that he found it at the end of his trip. Maybe we can accept that. Ulak could be as many as three days from here, and as far as we know his Indian guides turned back. We can look at the Ulak days as time spent prospecting and collecting clues."

Chris paused and gathered his thoughts. "But then you have to ask another question: why did Morde keep saying in the press that the city was between the Paulaya and the Plátano?"

Another diversion, I guessed.

"Maybe, but here's another way to think about it. If you look at a map, this site, by longitude and latitude, is actually between the headwaters of those two rivers. There's a lot of land between there. A lot. It's just a very broad interpretation, which would allow him to tell the truth." He stopped as I wrote this down. "The truth," he said, "but not the whole truth."

We munched Clif Bars and walked to the other end of the temple. "He probably would never have found this without a guide. That's the last part. He would have had to convince someone not only to tell him but also to bring him here." Chris paused. "Of course, he could also have totally stumbled into this place by pure luck."

"Luck?"

"That's how things are discovered sometimes. Luck."

I wondered what this place would have looked like around seventy years ago, when Morde was here.

"It would have been completely covered in jungle. All those trails we walked would have been even more treacherous and muddy. This site would be almost impenetrable. But a guide could show him. That's what I think happened."

"What about the gold?"

Chris chuckled. "If there was any gold here, it was taken a long time ago."

▼　▼　▼

THE SIGNIFICANCE OF Morde's walking stick remained a problem for us. What exactly did it mean?

No matter how much we toiled over the question, Chris and I kept hitting a snag: if the coordinates running down the four sides of the stick were supposed to be directions to a significant place, where was the starting point? We needed more information.

It would be only later, after leaving Honduras, that I'd get some answers from a man named Derek Parent. Parent had been thinking about the issue of the walking stick for a long time. A Canadian spatial analyst and cartographer specializing in mapping indigenous traditional knowledge, Parent was also the author of a technical guidebook and digital navigation maps of the Mosquitia region. In the decades that he had been obsessing over the White City legend, he had scoured old archives in Honduras, the University of Texas Institute of Latin American Studies library, and the Perry-Castañeda Library Map Collection, as well as bushwhacked through the forest. "I did jungle excursions two or three times a year," he told me on the phone one morning. "I walked in water up to my chest for six or seven hours a day. Many times I walked tens of kilometers at night under the moonlight to avoid the oppressive heat and humidity." He said he was probably the first to ever kayak the entire Mosquito Coast. "Originally it was designed for the special forces of the British army," he snickered. "The locals thought it was a submarine."

Parent had also spent about ten years talking and theorizing with Morde's nephew Dave in North Carolina. It was Dave who introduced us. Using Morde's stick notations, Parent told me, he'd mapped more than a dozen different possibilities for the lost-city site. When we talked about that process, he called it "following the squiggle," referring to the waving, doodling path that resulted from laying down the stick's instructions—including bearings, as on a compass, and distance, as in a man's stride—on one of his highly technical custom maps of the Honduran jungle.

As he saw it, the stick's first instruction, NE 300, was straightforward: walk northeast 300 strides, followed by E 150, meaning you were to pivot to the east and trek for another 150 steps—and so on for the stick's thirty-three moves. Interestingly, the stick also noted a couple topographical references, such as "CREEK RIGHT," providing the seeker at least some vague sense of the landscape.

Parent superimposed the squiggle on his map scale along the many miles of the winding Patuca and then up near Morde's Camp Ulak. Could the markings be a path to a gold-washing site? he wondered at one point. Still, no matter how many times he mapped the squiggle, none of the scenarios seemed exactly right. So he changed his approach. Maybe the numbers were not directions to or from a site but instead the measurements—in feet—of the site itself. He superimposed Morde's stick coordinates on a map of the Las Crucitas ruins. "Now, that was interesting," he told me. The stick coordinates traced some of the ancient wall structures protruding out of the jungle terrain. I said, "So Morde's stick is Las Crucitas!" Parent liked the theory too. It would be the closest I would get to solving the riddle of the walking stick.

▼ ▼ ▼

STILL A MYSTERY remained—one of the questions that had launched this journey in the first place: was Las Crucitas actually the legendary lost city also known as Ciudad Blanca?

Chris took a minute before answering, leaning down to tie his boot. In the distance I could see the gunman readying his mule to go. I slugged down my water and looked back at Chris, who now shook his head. "I'm sorry," he said. "It's not the White City."

"What do you mean?" I'd had visions of coming home to cameras, press wanting to hear about my White City discovery. "What about what the Tawahkas said?" I asked. "Do you just discount all of those stories and the people who pointed us to this site as the place?"

"It's more complicated than that," he said. "This isn't it." His tone was now definitive. He knew, having walked the region for years and discovered more than a hundred sites. "It's an amazing discovery. In Morde's time it would have been huge. It's probably the biggest site around here next to the Maya sites in the north." He paused, wiped his forehead with a shirtsleeve. "But it's not the White City."

That should have been the end of my journey. We were running low on food. We were all tired. I reeked. My clothes were in tatters. I missed my family. It was time to get the hell out of there. I began to walk back to the gunman and the mule. Then I stopped. Some urgent impulse sprang up in me. "Where is the White City, then?" I asked.

His answer was oblique as usual. "You need to see something," he said.

"What?"

"Trust me."

He said what he wanted to show me was three days' walking from here. Two days if we found a ride at some point. It had something to do with the riddle of the city. I tried to contemplate the trek but couldn't. "It's not what you expect," he said. I had no idea what to expect now. And I shouldn't have even thought of going farther. But I had to know, even though it was foolish.

THE LOST CITY

D o you know in the Bible when Jesus' disciples go out to sea on a boat and they are struck by a storm?" Pancho asked. We were bumping along a dirt logging track in the back of a mud-caked 4×4. "They didn't think they would make it out alive. They thought they were dead."

Before going on, we were taking Pancho to Bonanza—the village he had left behind some ten years before. We had gotten lucky with the pickup truck and were now heading west, after slogging for a day through the mountains. Pancho paused, probably remembering something that he didn't want to talk about yet.

"They were so afraid," he finally said, raising his hands at the wet green horizon. "And then Jesus said, 'Be still,' and everything was still. It is beautiful suddenly when the storm ends. That is Bonanza. That is the name of my old village. *Mucho* beauty and peace. It is *tranquillo.*"

The last two days it had rained and rained. Earlier in the afternoon, we had made a quick visit to an old Indian cacique whom Chris had known for many years. When Chris had told him where we were headed, the cacique had said that the secluded area of jungle was known as a "doorway," suggesting that it led to another reality.

He had never been there himself, but his grandfather and father had told him, "It is where the gods live. It is the White City."

The cacique said that the stories we had heard about the lost city were mistaken. "You can only go there if you know all the languages of our people," he said, wiping a drip of sweat from his creased cheek. "And if they let you in, you will never leave. They don't let you come and then go." Chris smiled as if to say, the riddle only deepens.

The dirt roads went up and down through the hills of Olancho, and as we got closer to Bonanza, the rain ceased and the afternoon air was cooling. I couldn't stop thinking about Pancho's past. Why does a man flee a place he loves? What happened? And what would he find there now?

Pancho had switched off his radio and mostly stared off at the fog-draped treetops, perhaps bracing for what was to come. There was no news on the coup. President Mel Zelaya was still promising an armed return, and the rebel government was still promising to squash him if he tried. Months would pass before the end of the curfews, the protesting, and the general unrest. It wouldn't be until the fall that Mel would secretly return to Honduras, holing up in the Brazilian embassy. But he never returned to power. He would eventually concede the election of a new president and then fly into exile in the Dominican Republic, where he would complain that the United States had been against him all along.

▼ ▼ ▼

THE SUN WAS falling when we arrived in Bonanza, a village of about a dozen shacks flung over a few hills. Stepping out of the truck, Pancho, in his blue perma-pressed shirt, paused on the wet ground, as if to get his footing, and looked up at the rising pale half-moon. He then walked us down a mud-slicked path to meet his sister. The three-room house was built next to a wide stream, surrounded by tall cocoa plants and corn stalks that creaked in the early-evening breeze. When he walked in, Pancho took off his hat and his sister threw her arms around him. There were elated shouts from nieces and nephews, who swarmed him and Angel. There were hours of reminiscing and laughing. Later, I could hear a man at a tiny church on the hill singing "It's the Word, the Word is here" in the quiet air. For dinner, Pancho's sister's husband killed a chicken, and in the yellow candlelight his smiling face glowed. It was as though he had never left.

We spent the night on the porch in hammocks, and the next morning Pancho borrowed a .22-caliber rifle. It seemed to me that we had made it this far without a gun and could finish the journey without one. But Pancho was insistent. After black coffee and rice, we said good-bye to his family, and Pancho, wearing his perfect blue button-down shirt, led us twenty minutes up a muddy path to a two-story shack with a tin roof.

"My house," he said, stepping up to a wood fence. There were no other places in sight. "I built that with my hands." We stood there until a man—the new owner—emerged with a rifle, and then we continued on.

Farther uphill, Pancho pointed out a dilapidated shack in an overgrown pasture. "That was once our school," he said. "I built that too."

He bit his lip and looked at his hands. At one time, Angel, his two brothers, and thirty-seven other Bonanza kids had taken classes there. But now the wood walls were warping and peeling away, the roof was coming undone, and the jungle grass had begun to devour it. "It is all gone," he said.

Earlier, I hadn't felt comfortable pressing him about why he had left Bonanza, but now seemed like the right time. I had talked about what I left behind in New York, about my searching, about my life. We had come to know each other, even become friends. When I asked, Pancho looked at Angel as if to make sure his son didn't mind.

"There were once sixteen houses in this part of the village," he began, staring off at the wall of forest surrounding us. "Now there are none." He walked on, the rifle slung over one shoulder. "It started when the bandits came. They said they wanted the land, but we said no, and they kept coming back with their guns." He stopped, took off his hat, and wiped his forehead with the back of his hand. "When we said no, the bandits tried to take our girls away."

I wasn't sure that I had heard him right, so I asked what he meant. "They said they were going to take some of the village girls away if we didn't give them the land. They wanted to scare us, but we stopped them," he said.

He squeezed his eyes shut, as though he was fighting back emotions that were contorting his face. It was the first time that I had seen him look so vulnerable since our scare driving across Bandit Alley at the trip's start.

"There was a shoot-out," he said, kneeling at a stream to fill up his water bottle. "Two of the bandits were killed. The leader of the village also died."

I asked if he had been responsible for killing the two bad men, but he didn't answer in a straightforward way, and I didn't push him. "I was involved in the dispute," he said.

"So why did you leave?"

"We feared that there would be more killings, so I left."

"What about the other bandits?" I asked. "Did they keep coming back?"

He looked back at the path that led to Bonanza, as if to suggest that they lived there now, but he didn't elaborate. When I asked Chris about it later, he didn't fully understand the conclusion of the story either.

There was one last thing that Pancho needed to do before we moved on. He wanted to see his son, Francisco Noel, who had died of asthma when he was seventeen months old. Were he alive today, the little boy would be a teenager. But in Pancho's mind, he remained a child, with large blinking eyes and little feet. The day he died, Pancho had carried his tiny body to a small field of high razor grass three hours by foot from Bonanza. With a shovel, he had dug a hole and buried his baby son. He hadn't marked the grave with a headstone. Instead, he had planted yellow vine flowers that now crowned the grass like a necklace.

As Chris and I hung back, Pancho and Angel walked into the field, found the grave, and knelt to the ground. Pancho put his hands to his face and leaned downward, as if to get closer to the son he had buried in the earth so many years before. He spent close to half an hour there in silent conversation with his two sons, one living and one dead, among the yellow flowers.

When he returned to us, he was smiling. "Isn't it beautiful out here?" he said, the insects singing in the summer heat. *"Tranquillo."*

▼ ▼ ▼

WE HEADED WEST toward the Río Plátano. Morde's mysterious Trujillo source had spoken of a buried city somewhere around this river, "over high mountains, where there grow strange large flowers." Around here, the source had also mentioned a "burial ground."

"It's not much farther," Chris said after hours of walking through tangled and muddy terrain. "We should make it by night."

By now we had entered a swath of protected jungle, called the Río Plátano Biosphere Reserve: 3,262 square miles of mostly undisturbed and roadless mountains, valleys, rivers, and swamps—about the size of Delaware and Rhode Island combined. A UNESCO World Heritage Site, the reserve is also mostly uninhabited, except for the indigenous who come to hunt and the narcos who operate in its unreachable shadows.

Chris led us, occasionally pulling out his GPS to check coordinates. Trees climbed ten and fifteen stories high, their heavy canopies alive with noise. Occasionally I looked down and noticed more stones imprinted with strange shapes. The jungle grew so deep and dark that at times I couldn't see Chris or Pancho in front of me, and I felt as if I had been swallowed up. Even though the sun was still out, it felt like evening under the trees, and everything was in shadow. On a descent into a valley, Pancho swung his machete at the ground and killed a coral snake. Another time, we barely missed stepping into a nest of bullet ants. Pancho reared back and threw his arms out. Although there were hundreds of them, each about an inch long, I would never have seen them in the dark mud. Later, I would come across a pain scale—known as the Schmidt Sting Pain Index after its developer, the entomologist Justin O. Schmidt—that described the bullet ant's sting this way: "Pure, intense, brilliant. Like fire-walking over flaming charcoal with a 3-inch rusty nail grinding into your heel." Of all the jungle we'd walked so far, this was the most treacherous.

It was dark when we reached the Plátano, but a rainstorm forced us to stop. It came down with a fury that broke branches and made it almost impossible to see even with our headlamps switched on. In the wet darkness, Pancho said, "The ghosts are here." We climbed into our hammocks and tried to sleep.

In the morning, Chris said, "We'll have to swim the river. There's no other way." I could see the Plátano now, about thirty yards across and full of white rapids. It was impossible to know its depth.

Fully clothed, Chris stepped into the river and disappeared. My clothes were still wet from the storm; my bones ached as always. Having hardly slept, I looked at Angel, who shrugged, and then I walked into the water as if in a dream. Almost immediately, I was knocked down, pulled underwater, and thrown back first into a shoal of rocks. I felt my breath go as the water dragged me at least thirty yards downstream before I could snatch a vine and pull myself up the other side.

As I caught my breath, Chris appeared, pointed at the forest, and said, "So this is it."

I didn't see anything. "What's it?"

He chopped away some brush with his machete, and a three-foot-high cobblestone wall, covered in moss, appeared. "This way," he said. We followed it into the forest and stopped on a rock slab that was etched with various figures. "This is what I wanted to show you," he said.

"This is the White City?"

He smiled. "It's the first lost city that I discovered here. It's where this began for me," he said, gesturing at the forest around us.

"What?"

"This is where my understanding of Ciudad Blanca began."

"But what about the city?" I asked.

"Be patient," he said. "You see, when I started asking about the city's location, people told me different stories. The Pech have two or three versions of the city, and so do the Tawahka."

Chris had lived with the Pech for almost six years. "I came here and then found some other places that seemed like they could be the White City. So at first I thought, there's not one White City, but maybe there are multiple lost cities, any of which could be the White City. But then over the years I started to believe something else."

He paused to watch a troop of monkeys pass loudly overhead, branches and fruit dropping into space. "You're probably not going to like this."

I already didn't like it.

"Well, I started to believe that the White City was not actually a physical place."

Not a physical place? I wanted to grab him by the neck. Punch him in his glasses. We'd walked all the way out here, through the mud and the bush, with the mosquitoes and the snakes and the damn bullet ants. I'd almost died! "Are you serious?"

"I said you weren't going to like it."

I wondered if his head was on straight. I said he was starting to sound like the Pech chief and his "doorway" theory. I was tired of riddles.

He laughed. "Are you calm now?" he asked.

I nodded. He waited. I breathed. "Okay," I said, "I'm calm."

"The White City, in my mind, is not a literal place," he said now. "I think that it's a metaphor for what is lost—that is, what's been lost."

Like my youth, I thought for a moment. That gallivanting kid I was before Amy and I had had a child, bought a house, moved to Brooklyn. And the adult I was supposed to be, looking back on those lost days, once with nerves and a little sadness but now with something else like understanding. I had missed a lot back home. Sky wouldn't always be four. She wouldn't always care about my being around. In obsessing about what I'd lost, it was easy to forget about what had been gained in growing older—being a husband and a father. I saw it so clearly. I remember the first time I'd taken Sky on the spinning teacups ride at a festival in upstate New York. She was three, and, as the teacup car whipped around in quick, jerky circles, she screamed and screamed at the top of her lungs. When the cup came groaning to a stop, I thought for sure that she'd be crying. But she looked up at me, her hair a mess in her little face, and said, "I almost threw up, Daddy! Let's do that again!" There were other moments just like that, moments when my old world receded and I saw the world through her eyes, with surprise, with newness, as if its own discovery.

This was how Morde and I were different. Morde had tried to settle down, but he'd continued to itch and the itching had in part killed him. I understood the itch and that there would likely be other moments in life when the itch came on and I would have to deal with it. I knew it would be hard fighting it off. But as I stood there soaking wet, sleep deprived, and aching, I wanted to change more than anything. I needed to get out of here. In my notebook, I wrote, "You are so close. Go home."

Chris stuck his machete into the soft earth and gave me a look that said, stay with me. "For the indigenous people, it seems in general that the legend refers to the last areas in which these groups lived prior to being in close contact with other groups, like where they lived before the Spanish arrived. Essentially the White City is the place [in their memory] that no longer exists anymore—their lost frontier, their lost lives, their lost autonomy, the good old days. They believe in it because it represents the past that they don't want to forget." He stopped for a second and then added, "It is their story."

He motioned for us to walk on, and we made our way over the ruins, where he said that a thousand or so people had lived more than a thousand years ago. Then he continued with his theory. "The thing is, this lost city is no longer lost," he said.

What he seemed to mean was that it had been discovered (by him) and mapped (by him), just like Las Crucitas. "So in my opinion, that disqualifies it—it's important archaeologically, but it can no longer be the White City, because the White City must always be lost."

"So this is why you brought me all the way out here?" I said, half jokingly and still half not. "To show me something that isn't the White City?"

"Sort of," he said. "This is the story. You have to understand this."

It was around that time, just as I was starting to calm down, that I had a revelation about Morde. It had probably been bubbling up inside me for some time but only now made sense. What if he'd actually understood what Chris was talking about now and made a deliberate choice not to go back to the city? Like the indigenous people in Chris's telling, what if Morde, at some point after the war, after his life began to fall apart, suddenly recognized that his lost city had to remain untouched, that he couldn't give up the directions, that it had to stay a secret?

In Morde's time, the world was shrinking and frontiers were being lost. In the midst of war and upheaval, the popular imagination needed romance. What better romance was there than the continuing story of a great lost civilization, shrouded in foggy wilderness, inhabited by ghosts and monkey gods, with gold buried amid all the fetid green? It was a hopeful story for a darkly claustrophobic time—that there were still places to discover, that there was forgotten beauty somewhere out there. What if Morde hadn't gone back because he'd decided to protect what had been lost, while at the same time protecting his story, an unforgettably vibrant and freeing moment in his life? At no other time did he seem to be so alive, so young, so in need of being transformed again and again. I liked to believe that.

Just then Pancho came running out of the brush. He had an urgent look on his face. "You need to see this," he said, pointing through the trees.

We bushwhacked for half an hour or so until we stood in front of a white cliff. Rising steeply for about a hundred feet into the blue sky, the cliff was overgrown with trees and creepers and moss. It was pure white. Midway up, two caves, like eyes, had been carved out of the rock. Chris had never seen it before. "Damn," he said. "Now, this is interesting."

EPILOGUE

A FEW DAYS LATER, I was on a plane zipping back to New York, and then, after a connecting flight and a long cab ride from the airport through midafternoon traffic, I was standing on the sidewalk in front of my brownstone in Brooklyn. Moisture from the jungle had destroyed my cell phone, so I had not been able to call Amy and Sky to tell them when I'd be back. By now I had been gone for more than a month. As I stood there in the August heat, I thought, "Here you are."

It had taken us two days to trek out of the jungle and then another day in the back of a 4×4 pickup to get back to La Ceiba. Since then I had been processing everything that had happened, the stories of those days on playback, my brain trying to piece them all together— the Paris Hotel that first morning after landing when I'd had no idea how things would turn out, the Queens guy trying to meet up with his hotstuffie92, the dead motorcycle man in the road, the Geo Prizm busting up on Bandit Alley, the pirate named Frog, the old Indian Marcos, the man rushing to see his sick son, Pancho's homecoming, and, of course, Las Crucitas.

The images stuck with me as I turned the key in the lock and trudged up the two carpeted flights of stairs. My backpack was a lot lighter now, as I had given away the last of the food and dumped my jungle boots and ruined clothes. But it didn't matter much for my back, which still hurt from the weeks of walking. It would be months before I straightened it out again.

I pushed open the door, and there they were, the two of them, my girls. Finally. Sky screaming and Amy smiling. I could have held them all afternoon.

On the flight home, I had attempted to play out this reunion a million times, imagining the stories that I would tell and how Amy and Sky would respond, but I couldn't ever fully see it.

"I can't believe you're four," I said to Sky.

"Soon I'll be four and a half."

"Not if I can help it," I said.

In the bedroom, I noticed the duct-taped window and the ripped screen where the raccoon had attacked. "He's gone," Amy said.

"What do you mean?"

"A guy came with a trap and caught him."

"I'll fix the window," I said.

Amy leaned in to me, and I held her. She traced a finger down my bearded face and said, "Is that really you behind that?"

As I shaved later, I thought of Morde shaving away his beard, a man trying to scrape through the buildup to find himself. Adults, unlike children, are guided by memories, driven by them until they figure out how to contain them, live with them.

We ate pizza on the roof that night with the city skyline rising in front of us, and later we watched the sun sink over the East River. I kept thinking, "I'm home, I'm home." This was my return, probably the last one—at least for a long time.

Soon Sky climbed into my lap and nuzzled into my chest, and I knew what would come next. Amy leaned over the table toward us and sipped her wine. Her eyes were greener than I remembered.

At that moment, I could not imagine being anywhere else. I held her stare, and we were quiet for a bit, until Sky broke the silence.

"So, Daddy," she said, "tell me what you did in the jungle. Did you find what you were looking for?"

ACKNOWLEDGMENTS

Many people helped me along on this adventure, and there is no simple way to say thank you, especially in such limited space. But I will give it a shot.

The archaeologist Chris Begley led me through the Honduran jungle, picked me up when I fell down—and I fell a lot—and generally kept me alive, while answering a gazillion questions before, during, and long after the journey to find the famous Ciudad Blanca.

Dave Morde trusted me enough to hand over all of his uncle Theodore Morde's journals. Without Dave's generosity, this book would not have happened. Thank you also to his wife, Diana, for her e-mails when Dave was off doing other things—and I won't ever forget those chocolate-chip cookies.

A number of others of Morde's family also helped along the way, including Carol Ross, Joseph Essaye, Susan Shumway, and Joan Cenedella.

Early on in my research, I spoke to Jim Woodman, who told me many stories about his own adventures in the Honduran wilderness. I met him once in Miami for a good Honduran meal. Sadly, Jim died in 2011, before I could tell him thank you.

A Canadian mapmaker named Derek Parent wrote me scores of e-mails outlining his theories about Morde's discovery. He also provided extensive maps detailing Morde's journey and where the city might be. He was always there for me.

I'm thankful to Mike Burger and Kyle Pope, who put up with reading early drafts and helped me see around some hard corners.

Others who provided personal and professional support were Brett Forrest, Alexandra Jacobs, Andrew Goldman, Cary Goldstein, Chad Higginbotham, Karl Greenfield, Allison Lorentzen, Abraham Lustgarten, Andrew Rice, Aram Roston, Lockhart Steele, and Lloyd Taylor.

I'm indebted to P. J. Mark, the finest agent around. He has had my back from the beginning.

Julia Cheiffetz believed that I could actually pull this off before it was anything more than a totally far-fetched idea to go searching for a lost city.

Christian Lorentzen was absolutely vital early on in shaping the manuscript in almost every single way.

At Harper, David Hirshey and Barry Harbaugh ultimately carried this to the finish line. To them, I am most grateful. Their smart edits and steady counsel made the book better than it could have ever been otherwise. Yes, they're the greatest.

To Mom, Dad, and brother, DJ: thank you.

To Amy, my wife: you toughed out another book. You let me go on this crazy trip and then helped me see it through, even when you were long over it. But we did it. Obviously, I owe you big-time. Same with Sky, our daughter. I will never miss another birthday. That's a promise.

Finally, my son, Dash, is too young now, but the one thing I hope he takes away from this book when he reads it years from now is this: if given the choice between seeking a lost city in the jungle and not, always pick the jungle.

NOTES

In writing about Theodore Morde's quest to find the lost city, I relied on recollections from his family and, most important, his personal expedition papers. Altogether, there are some two hundred hand-written pages in his journals. Some sections are hard to read, and at times it is unclear if it is Morde writing a passage or Bob Burke or Laurence Brown, the two men who accompanied him on the months-long journey. To make it easier, I always attribute entries to Morde, as it was Morde's expedition and Morde's journals.

I consulted many news stories and magazine articles from the time around Morde's travels, most of which are cited in the text. Of the numerous books I read, Peter Keenagh's book *Mosquito Coast* was particularly useful in understanding what the Mosquitia looked like several years before Morde arrived in 1940. It is unfortunately out of print. Troy S. Floyd's *The Anglo-Spanish Struggle for Mosquitia* was also integral to my comprehension of the country's politics.

Once Morde entered the world of spies at the start of World War II, I leaned heavily on recently declassified government files. His letters regarding the details of the plot to build a clandestine group inside Germany to capture Hitler are now housed in the Franklin D. Roosevelt Presidential Library in Hyde Park, New York, but have been collected in part in the book *American Intelligence and the German Resistance to Hitler.*

Among the critical half-dozen sources I interviewed about the OSS was Robert Amman, whose uncle was in the service during the war. He helped me in particular to grasp the life of a U.S. agent overseas. Two books provided much historical insight, helping me shape some of the context for Morde's mission in Turkey and his later stints in Italy and China: Richard Harris Smith's *OSS: The Secret History of America's First Intelligence Agency* and Anthony Cave Brown's biography of OSS chief Bill Donovan.

Meanwhile, the more pedestrian details of Morde's life, both before his days as an explorer and following the war, come largely from Theodore's nephew Dave Morde and a handful of others in the Morde family, along with various news clippings, which I note throughout the book.

As for my trip, it is mostly a record of personal thoughts and observations, informed by the archaeologist Chris Begley and, at times, Pancho, my local lost-city hunter. For news about the Honduran coup, I read every major newspaper every day but learned much from the coverage in the *New York Times*, as well as from William Finnegan's lengthy story in the *New Yorker*. Some names of people I met along the way were changed to protect identities. Early on, I read a 1978 article in *Sports Illustrated* called "Quest in the Jungle." It helped me understand the dangers of the jungle and what others had found there in their searches for the White City.

Books by Betty Meggers and Jared Diamond helped me understand the possibilities—or impossibilities—of human life in the jungle. David Grann's book *The Lost City of Z* was also instructive.

Before I left for Honduras, William V. Davidson, a former professor of anthropology at Louisiana State University, provided a key piece of the lost-city legend—a translation of Bishop Pedraza's letter to the Spanish emperor about standing on a rise in the jungle with an Indian princess who told him of a land beyond the horizon, where nobles smelted gold.

BIBLIOGRAPHY

Adams, Mark. *Turn Right at Machu Picchu: Rediscovering the Lost City One Step at a Time*. New York: Plume, 2012.

Binns, Jack R. *The United States in Honduras, 1980–1981*. Jefferson, N.C.: McFarland, 2000.

Boorstin, Daniel. *The Discoverers: A History of Man's Search to Know His World and Himself*. New York: Random House, 1983.

Brown, Anthony Cave. *The Last Hero: Wild Bill Donovan*. New York: Times Books, 1982.

Childress, David Hatcher. *Lost Cities and Ancient Mysteries of South America*. Stelle, Ill.: Adventures Unlimited Press, 1986.

Cohen, Rich. *Israel Is Real: An Obsessive Quest to Understand the Jewish Nation an.d Its History*. New York: Farrar, Straus and Giroux, 2009.

Cortes, Fernando. *Letters of Cortes*. New York: G. P. Putnam's Sons, 1908.

Diamond, Jared. *Collapse: How Societies Choose to Fail or Succeed*. New York: Viking, 2005.

———. *Guns, Germs, and Steel: The Fates of Human Societies*. New York: W. W. Norton, 1999.

Environmental Investigation Agency. "The Illegal Logging Crisis in Honduras: How U.S. and E.U. Imports of Illegal Honduran

Wood Increase Poverty, Fuel Corruption and Devastate Forests and Communities." London: EIA, 2005.

Finnegan, William. "An Old-Fashioned Coup." *New Yorker*, November 30, 2009.

Fleming, Peter. *Brazilian Adventure*. Evanston, Ill.: Marlboro Press, 1999.

Floyd, Troy S. *The Anglo-Spanish Struggle for Mosquitia*. Albuquerque: University of New Mexico Press, 1967.

Ford, Peter. *Tekkin a Waalk: Along the Miskito Coast*. New York: HarperCollins, 1991.

Grann, David. *The Lost City of Z: A Tale of Deadly Obsession in the Amazon*. New York: Doubleday, 2009.

Grimes, William. "The Indian Museum's Last Stand." *New York Times Magazine*, November 27, 1988.

Heideking, Jurgen, and Christof Mauch. *American Intelligence and the German Resistance to Hitler: A Documentary History*. New York: Westview Press, 1996.

Hemming, John. *The Search for El Dorado*. London: Book Club Association, 1978.

Keenagh, Peter. *Mosquito Coast: An Account of a Journey Through the Jungles of Honduras*. Boston: Houghton Mifflin, 1938.

Lapper, Richard. *Honduras: State for Sale*. London: Latin America Bureau, 1985.

Mann, Charles C. *1491: New Revelations of the Americas Before Columbus*. New York: Alfred A. Knopf, 2005.

Meggers, Betty J. *Amazonia: Man and Culture in a Counterfeit Paradise*. Washington, D.C.: Smithsonian Institute Press, 1996.

Naipaul, V. S. *The Loss of El Dorado: A Colonial History*. New York: Vintage, 2003.

Nicholls, Mark. *Sir Walter Raleigh: In Life and Legend*. London: Continuum, 2011.

Norsworthy, Kent, and Tom Barry. *Inside Honduras*. Albuquerque, N.M.: Interhemispheric Resource Center, 1994.

O'Donnell, Patrick K. *Operatives, Spies, and Saboteurs: The Unknown Story of the Men and Women of World War II's OSS.* New York: Free Press, 2004.

Outhwaite, Leonard. *Unrolling the Map: The Story of Exploration.* New York: John Day, 1972.

Preston, Douglas. "The Lost City." *New Yorker,* October 20, 1997.

Smith, Richard Harris. *OSS: The Secret History of America's First Central Intelligence Agency.* Guilford, Conn.: Lyons Press, 2005.

Striffer, Steve, and Mark Moberg. *Banana Wars: Power, Production, and History in the Americas.* Durham, N.C.: Duke University Press, 2003.

Theroux, Paul. *The Mosquito Coast.* Boston: Houghton Mifflin, 1984.

———. *The Old Patagonian Express: By Train Through the Americas.* New York: Penguin, 1980.

Trevelyan, Raleigh. *Sir Walter Raleigh: Being a True and Vivid Account of the Life and Times of the Explorer, Soldier, Scholar, Poet, and Courtier— the Controversial Hero of the Elizabethan Age.* New York: Henry Holt, 2004.

Underwood, John. "Quest in the Jungle." *Sports Illustrated,* January 9, 1978.

Wallace, Kevin. "Slim-Shin's Monument." *New Yorker,* November 19, 1960.

Waller, Douglas. *Wild Bill Donovan: The Spymaster Who Created the OSS and Modern American Espionage.* New York: Free Press, 2011.

Wilford, John Noble. *The Mapmakers.* New York: Alfred A. Knopf, 1981.

ABOUT THE AUTHOR

CHRISTOPHER S. STEWART is a writer and editor at the *Wall Street Journal*. His work has appeared in *GQ*, *Harper's*, *New York*, the *New York Times Magazine*, the *Paris Review*, *Wired*, and other publications. He is also the author of *Hunting the Tiger: The Fast Life and Violent Death of the Balkans' Most Dangerous Man*. He lives with his family in Brooklyn.